PENGUIN BOOKS

# ALTAR BOY

Andrew Madden lives in Dublin and works as a freelance IT consultant.

# Altar Boy

## *A Story of Life After Abuse*

ANDREW MADDEN

PENGUIN BOOKS

PENGUIN BOOKS

Published by the Penguin Group
Penguin Ireland Ltd, 25 St Stephen's Green, Dublin 2, Ireland
Penguin Books Ltd, 80 Strand, London WC2R ORL, England
Penguin Group (USA) Inc., 375 Hudson Street, New York, New York 10014, USA
Penguin Books Australia Ltd, 250 Camberwell Road, Camberwell, Victoria 3124, Australia
Penguin Books Canada Ltd, 10 Alcorn Avenue, Toronto, Ontario, Canada M4V 3B2
Penguin Books India (P) Ltd, 11 Community Centre, Panchsheel Park, New Delhi – 110 017, India
Penguin Books (NZ) Ltd, Cnr Rosedale and Airborne Roads, Albany, Auckland, New Zealand
Penguin Books (South Africa) (Pty) Ltd, 24 Sturdee Avenue, Rosebank 2196, South Africa

Penguin Books Ltd, Registered Offices: 80 Strand, London WC2R ORL, England

www.penguin.com

First published by Penguin Ireland 2003
Published in Penguin Books 2004
1

Copyright © Andrew Madden, 2003
All rights reserved

The moral right of the author has been asserted

Set by Rowland Phototypesetting Ltd, Bury St Edmunds, Suffolk
Printed in England by Clays Ltd, St Ives plc

Thanks . . .

. . . To my family for all their love and support. To Alan, Phil, Noel, Declan, Des and others for their friendship. To Val Devlin for always being there. To the late Father Duffy for surrounding me with so many new friends at a difficult time. To Mayanie for forgiving me, love always. To Cabaret Voltaire for bringing Tony Ward to my attention. To Helen Smith and John Briden for friendship and understanding during awful times. To Ann for listening. To Penguin Ireland for saying yes. To Patricia Deevy for editing.

And finally to Daniel: *I Will Always Love You . . .*

# Contents

# 1. Altar Boy

Sunday morning was my favourite time of the week. My altar boy's red soutane and white surplice were freshly washed and ironed by my mother and I carried them round to the church, careful not to crease them. The small roads around Cabra were busy with people coming from the earlier Mass. I was happier serving at the eleven or twelve o'clock Mass. There were more people and there was nearly always music. Miss Curran played the organ and I loved it when everyone sang along to 'Soul of My Saviour' and 'Holy God, We Praise Thy Name'.

I passed through the large black gates of the church where a red-faced old man sold newspapers. The sacristy had a special feel about it. The priests spent a lot of time in a room of their own where they changed into vestments and got ready for Mass. Terry, the church clerk, was the only one allowed to go in and out of that room without knocking. A tall thin man with grey hair and dark tinted glasses, Terry was in charge of us altar boys. He usually told us what Mass we had to serve the following Sunday and whether we had any funerals or weddings to do during the week. If I was asked to serve at a wedding I felt I was being given a treat: they were special occasions and we got paid for doing them – extra pocket money.

Christ The King church was huge. Walking out on to the altar with two or three other altar boys followed by the priest made me a bit nervous but I still enjoyed it. The people in the church stood up because the priest was so holy and important. Nobody made the sign of the cross until he did and then the Mass began. Each altar boy had his own job. My favourite was holding the paten under people's chins while the priest gave them Holy Communion. Other jobs were handing the priest a finger-bowl and towel after he had raised the large host and chalice during the prayer 'Blessed Are You, Lord God of All Creation'. Or sometimes we had to lift the back of the priest's outer vestment over the back of his chair as he sat down so it didn't crease. But holding the paten during Communion meant walking with the priest, sometimes quite far down the church, and staying with him until everyone had been given Communion. Lots of altar boys wanted that job on Sunday mornings but I usually turned up first and got it. Neighbours, friends and others got to see me with the priest up close. I felt good.

The priests of the parish seemed to be from a different world. They were all old – at least, older than my father. Their black suits, long black coats and collars made them stand out from everyone else I knew. My father's fireman's uniform, which I saw only on special occasions, looked good, but the priests looked special. Even Terry tiptoed through the sacristy when the priests were around. Some of them were friendlier than others. Father McDowell and Father Quigley hardly ever spoke to us, while Father Stokes always asked us how we were and gave us a big smile as he thanked us for serving Mass. Father Supple called at our house a few times. Usually it was late in the evening so my brother and sister, Stephen and Audrey, and I had gone to bed. At Christmas he would call a meeting of all the altar boys in the sacristy and he and Terry would call out our names and give us each a present of a box of chocolates. A present from Father Supple was something to be proud of. When friends and neighbours came into the house over Christmas I made sure to show them if they asked what presents I got: 'Look what Father Supple gave me.'

I was only eleven but I was really interested in the priests as they said Mass. I didn't understand much of what was going on. I made do with watching their different styles, observing the way they liked to wear their vestments. Father Supple wore his tightly, while the others had a looser, fuller sort of look which I preferred. At home I wrapped myself in sheets off my bed and played at being a priest in front of my dressing-table. I read from a leaflet picked up from a church seat and used cups and mugs for a chalice and the silver bowls used to carry the Holy Communion. I couldn't wait to do it for real.

I went to primary school at St Mary's Christian Brothers off Dorset Street. Everyone was into football and other sports which I didn't care for. The schoolwork didn't seem too hard and most of us enjoyed an easy time of it, so when it came to moving on to secondary school we knew we were in trouble. I failed the entrance exam into St Declan's College on Nephin Road. I repeated sixth class at St John Bosco's on the Navan Road. I made new friends but the teachers were more strict than I had been used to and I worried about my homework in a way I hadn't done before. Friends at my old school had been used to my stutter, though some of the other boys did make jokes. Now I had to start again with a whole new crowd. But the strict atmosphere in class meant nobody was going to laugh at me when I tried to read, and I was happy about that.

I was quiet. Football didn't interest me and I wasn't in a gang. I liked having one or two friends – Richard Tracey and Karl Curtis in school and Raymond Rooney at home. Our next-door neighbour, Peter Rogers, was a middle-aged man who bred canaries in an aviary in his back garden. Raymond already had budgies so Peter gave me my first pair of canaries and I started to breed them in a long cage in the garage. I called them George and Mildred, after the programme on the telly, and they had lots of baby birds over two years.

'You'll have to look after them properly,' Peter said.

'I will.'

'It's hard work cleaning out those cages,' he said.

'No problem.'

'Although the hen and cock are separate now, you'll have to put them together before they'll have any chicks.'

'Why?'

'You just do,' he said, winking at my father. I felt my cheeks turn pink. They obviously knew something I didn't.

Mostly Raymond and I just played on the street around the corner with Audrey and her friends. For Christmas 1976 I got a new bike so I spent a lot of time cycling around on my own. I loved going into town, picking up bird seed in Whacker's pet shop off Parnell Square, and cycling home again. My mother used to tell me to be careful on the bike and to come straight home. I had been in the Cubs and now I was in the Scouts but left as soon as I could. The uniform had cost a bomb so my mother wasn't too pleased. But the other boys seemed rougher and tougher than me and I felt very different from them. I didn't curse as much as they did and they were usually better than me at any games that had to be played. I couldn't wait to get out. Just before I did, another Scout's mother died. She lived locally and we had to do a guard of honour at the gates of Christ The King. Terry spotted me and asked me to serve at the funeral. I was glad that the Scouts got to see me doing something I was good at before I left.

Early the following year things started changing quickly. My parents split up and my father moved into a flat near our house. I missed him a lot even though I still got to see him at weekends. Sometimes he was waiting outside school to drive me home, which was great. I had worked hard at Bosco's and knew I would be accepted into St Declan's – maybe even the A class. Then Peter Rogers next door died suddenly. It was the first time I knew anyone who died. He had been so friendly and nice with children in the area and he helped me with my canaries. I felt very sad and missed him for a long time. His elderly mother was left living alone and I went in to see her every day after school and during the summer holidays. I helped with little jobs around the house and got her messages in the shop. If there was nothing to be done I just kept her company until one of her nieces came to stay in the evening.

Things were changing around at the church as well. Some of the older priests were leaving the parish and new priests were coming to take their place. Father Finn was young and had black hair and looked nice. He wore casual navy trousers and a navy cardigan or coat – no black suit. Father Dooley was almost as casual, though he didn't have Father Finn's good looks. Father Payne was the other new priest. He hardly wore black at all and had a foreign accent – American or Canadian, I thought. His hair was going grey and he looked as though he had had acne but he still seemed young.

I watched the new priests just as much as I had the older ones. Father Finn never bothered to tie the ropey belt – which Terry taught me was called a cincture – around his waist, so his vestments went all the way down to the ground and covered his feet. Father Dooley was tall, so about six inches of black trousers showed at the end of his vestments. As I had grown since becoming an altar boy my red soutane was shorter than I liked and my mother let it down a bit so that it covered the end of my trousers. I wondered if I should show Father Dooley – give him the hint. I decided not to. He was still quite new and didn't really know me. Both Father Finn and Father Dooley said Mass in a very ordinary way. Father Payne seemed ordinary enough too, at least at the beginning, apart from his accent.

I was still on my summer holidays when Terry came up to me one Sunday morning.

'Would you be interested in serving eight o'clock morning Mass for the next week, Andrew?'

'Yes, I would – but how come?' It was unusual for morning Masses during the week to have altar boys.

'Father Payne is covering for one of the other priests who's going on holiday and said he would like to have altar boys if any of you were interested.'

I'd need to make sure it was all right at home but apart from that I told Terry I'd do it. I had talked to Father Payne quite a few times since he came to our parish and he was very friendly. He had just changed his bright blue Fiat 124 for a very stylish metallic grey Renault 12 Automatic and had promised to take me for a drive in it some day. Like the other new priests he talked in an ordinary way, not religious-sounding like Father Supple. He asked questions about school and what we were doing on our holidays. He was interested in us and I looked forward to impressing him by turning up to serve at his morning Mass. All the other kids would probably be still in bed.

'Hi, Andrew,' said Father Payne, 'and how are you this morning?'

'Fine, thank you, and how are you?' I said.

'I'm fine. Listen, thanks very much for coming to serve – you're very good.'

'That's okay.'

'No, really, you're a great kid,' he said, and he gently tossed my hair.

Another altar boy, Tony, turned up as well. I wished he hadn't. Now the two of us looked good and not just me.

Father Payne thanked us again after Mass and we told him yes, we'd be back again tomorrow. After serving Mass for another few mornings Father Payne said he would take us down to his house for breakfast after we had been so good. He planned it for the next day. And he told us to make sure to 'clear it with your folks'.

It was great being in the new car. Nobody I knew had such a nice car. And out of all the priests of the parish Father Payne's was the nicest, and he drove fast, which I loved. He had a big red-brick house across the road from the Botanic Gardens and took us to the kitchen at the back. At home I usually had Weetabix for breakfast. Father Payne made boiled eggs and toast and swore as the pot boiled over on to his cooker.

'Oh, balls!'

'Now now, Father,' said Tony. 'There's no need to be using bad language.'

'I know,' said Father Payne grinning. 'But sometimes you just can't help it. You must swear sometimes – no?'

'No, not really.'

'Not even at school?'

'Sometimes, but not really that much,' said Tony.

'What about you, Andrew? What swear words do you use?'

'I don't swear either,' I said.

He didn't believe either of us.

I enjoyed the morning. Father Payne wasn't wearing his collar and even though we were in the priest's house it was easy to relax. Later he drove us home and said we would do the same another time. Terry had already asked if I would serve Father Payne's morning Mass for a second week. It was coming near the end of the summer holidays but I said yes anyway. The priest had been so nice and friendly it was impossible to say no. I only had a few weeks left before going on to secondary school. I would have less time to spend in the church then, so I wanted to enjoy it while I could. Tony had had enough after one week so I had Father Payne's attention all to myself. He drove me to his house another morning after Mass. He made breakfast and later I helped wash the dishes.

'You're very good at doing the dishes.'

'Well, I usually wash up nearly every night at home so I'm used to it.'

'I suppose you help out quite a lot at home.'

'Well, we all have our little jobs to do.'

'Do you get pocket money or do you just do it to help out?'

'Just to help out.'

'You really are very good kids, all three of you. If I needed some jobs done around the house, would you be interested in helping me? Of course, I'll pay you. I wouldn't expect you to do it for nothing.'

'Well, yes, I'd love to, but you wouldn't have to pay me.'

I was embarrassed by the offer of money but Father Payne insisted I would be paid and I was delighted. I just had to make sure it was all right at home. He put his arms around me from behind and hugged me for a long time. Father Supple had hugged my sister and me in the sacristy on the day he left Cabra. That was embarrassing enough. This was worse.

'Have you any tickles?' he asked, moving his hands under my arms.

'No, not really.' I found it hard not to laugh.

He carried on moving his hands around my chest, arms and down on to my legs. I laughed a lot.

'Do you fancy watching some TV before you go home?' he asked.

'Okay.'

The lounge was to the front of the house with a sliding door leading to the dining-room where there was a big piano.

I sat on the sofa. Father Payne turned on the television and sat beside me. Straight away he put his arm around my shoulders. I felt hot and uncomfortable.

'Are you all right?'

'Yes, fine,' I said. I couldn't think of what else to say. I was too embarrassed to say no. We watched football and Father Payne asked me what other programmes I liked to watch. At the same time his hands moved below my waist and moved slowly on to my private parts from outside my trousers. All the time I just watched the television. I was hot and felt sure my face had gone red. He said nothing for a while.

'Shall I drive you home?'

'Well, I don't mind walking.'

'No, no, I'll drive you up, it'll only take me a couple of minutes.'

I went home and did whatever jobs I had to do around the house that day so I could go out to play later. I thought about what had happened and I felt strange.

*What had just happened?*

Had I got it wrong? Maybe it was a mistake and he didn't mean it. He was different, after all. Look at his clothes, grey trousers and bright summer shirts. Look at his fast car. The way he drove. And the Yankee accent. Maybe he was just more friendly than people I was used to. I served Father Payne's Masses for the rest of the week and nothing happened. He was friendly and thanked me every day. Apart from Father Stokes the other priests never came to thank the altar boys before they went home. Some of the older priests who had left the parish didn't even know our names.

## 2. Saturdays on Botanic Road

I told my parents I had a new Saturday job working in Father Payne's garden. They said okay, but I had to make sure it did not get in the way of homework when I started secondary school. And I had to make sure I cleaned the garage and kept the birds' cages clean as usual.

On Sunday morning Father Payne came into the sacristy. He had been helping to give out Communion and was wearing his long white alb. The other priests wore a black soutane and white surplice when they were helping out with Communion. But Father Payne was different.

'Are you serving twelve o'clock Mass?' he said, looking at his watch.

'Hi, Father Payne, yes I am.'

'There's plenty of time, shall we go for a walk in the grounds for a few minutes?'

I should have been helping Terry get the altar ready but I preferred Father Payne's offer. People would be impressed when they saw the priest spending time with me.

'Quick, Christopher, here's the priest, now do what you're told or he'll give out to you,' a mother said to her son when she saw us walking around outside. The little boy looked at us and ran to his mother.

'Stupid parents,' Father Payne said to me quietly. 'If they keep telling children things like that they'll think priests are something to be afraid of. How do they ever expect the kids to talk to us if that's the way they carry on?'

'I don't know.'

'So are you coming to help with gardening next Saturday?'

'Oh yes, definitely, what time?'

'Come down at about one-thirty and we'll work for about three hours.'

I cycled down to 159 Botanic Road in Glasnevin and we started work in the back garden. Outside the kitchen door there was a shed full of jars of fruit left there for years by old people who had lived in the house before Father Payne. He was emptying each jar into a hole he had dug. He wanted to wash and save the empty jars. He looked even less like a priest than usual. His gardening clothes were older and dirtier than anything I'd seen him in. We didn't have dirty old clothes at home.

'Your clothes look very clean, are you sure they're okay for gardening?' he said.

'Yeah, they're fine.'

'I doubt if I have anything that will fit you but I can have a look if you'd like and you can change.'

'No, no, I'm fine really, thanks, these will do just fine.'

'Anything of mine would probably just be falling off you anyway.'

That was like something he said one day when we were leaving the sacristy. It was a hot day and he said I was probably just wearing enough clothes to cover myself. I remembered that because I thought it was a strange thing to say. And now he was inviting me to change out of my clothes. I had never done that anywhere apart from at home or at the beach with my family.

We worked for the rest of the afternoon in the hot sunshine. Father Payne gave me lemonade to keep cool and at about half past four he said we had done enough. He told me I could use the bathroom upstairs to clean up. I went inside and locked the door. The bathroom was clean with a shower over the bath. I wished we had a shower at home. I washed my hands and face in the sink and went back downstairs. Father Payne went upstairs to wash and change.

'I've left the television on for you, I'll be down in a minute.'

I went into the lounge and sat on the sofa where I had sat the last time. If I sat on a chair on my own Father Payne might think I had noticed something and was avoiding it. Better to carry on as if I hadn't. He came back to the room quickly and sat beside me.

'What's on?' he said.

'Just wrestling and an old black and white film.'

'What would you like to watch?'

'I don't mind.'

He put his arm around my shoulders again, asking if I was tired. He pulled me closer to him so he could rest his hands on my private parts more easily. I felt hot and sweaty as he moved his hand around more than the last time. Still his hand was outside my trousers. After a couple of minutes he stopped and asked me if I was ready to go home. He paid me nearly one pound fifty and I left. One pound fifty to myself. Apart from helping Peter Rogers with a paper-round on Sunday mornings, when my brother went away to the Gaeltacht, this was the first real money I'd had to myself. I climbed up and put it under a luminous statue of Our Lady which stood on top of my wardrobe. Mrs Rogers had given it to me as a present and it gave off a tiny shine when the bedroom was dark. I hated the dark and hated having to go upstairs on my own. Sometimes at night my mother asked me to go up and turn on her electric blanket. After I'd switched off the light in her room I ran down the stairs as fast as I could to get away from the dark bedrooms behind me.

What was Father Payne doing? What should I do? What

could I do? Who would I tell? What could I tell them anyway? What words could I use?

In early September I started at St Declan's. I wore grey trousers and shirt with a wine jumper and a blue and yellow tie. Coming from Bosco's meant there were fellas in my class that I knew already – Tony McCauley and Brendan Foster joined first year at the same time. Even so, it was my first day in a new school and I was nervous as I cycled up through Cabra West. My brother had been at Declan's for over a year and he brought home lots of homework, so I knew it wasn't going to be easy. It was a Christian Brothers' school and they lived in a big, newish-looking house in the grounds. Brother Bourke was in charge.

The first few days went well. I could cycle home at lunchtime and change books for afternoon classes. I looked through my new school books and at all the new subjects and couldn't imagine how I was going to learn everything. But I found I could keep up with the work during the day and the homework was okay as well.

The classroom was one of four small huts across the yard from the main school building. I sat beside Paul McGuinness, who was taller than me, with tight, curly hair and a big grin on his face most of the time. It was different to have a change of teacher for every subject. At least if there was any of them I didn't like I wouldn't have to see them for very long. Mostly they were lay teachers – all men.

'Shhh! Shhh! Here he is, here he is!' We ran to our seats as quick as we could. No one wanted to be the last one left standing up when the door opened. One of the few Brothers we had teaching us was on his way. He was at least fifty, short with grey hair and he wore his habit long with the half collar that Christian Brothers wear. I couldn't understand why they didn't go all the way and become priests. He asked everyone's name and told us he would always call us by our first name.

'When other teachers ask me about a certain boy – Whelan in 2A or Hoey in 1C – I always ask, "What's his first name?" Much nicer to call someone by their first name.'

On Saturday I went back to Father Payne's house. I was worried about my first weekend's homework so I did it all on the Friday when I came home from school. I helped him pull weeds and cut the grass while he messed around in the small glass-house beside the shed at the end of the garden.

'So how's everything in Declan's?' he said.

'Well, it's okay so far.'

'What are the other guys like?'

'Well, I knew some of them already and the rest are okay.'

'How's Audrey getting on in her new school?'

'She's not in a new school, she's just gone into the secondary part of the school she was already in, King's Inns Street.'

Father Payne sat beside me again later. The television was on. It was wrestling – it always seemed to be wrestling on a Saturday. I nearly said I was in a hurry home but chickened out at the last minute. 'Hurrying home for what?' he might have said.

I didn't think I could really stutter through a lie without him being able to tell. His arm was already around me and he moved his hand down like he had the other days. He stopped at the top of my trousers. Then he moved both of us about a bit as if he was just trying to get more comfortable. At the same time he moved his hand down inside my trousers resting on my private parts. I stared at the television. He didn't speak. He moved my underpants aside and took my private parts in his hand. My heart was racing and I was sure my face was red.

After a few minutes he took his hand out and put his arm around me.

'I'll just use the bathroom before I head home,' I said.

'Yeah, sure.'

When I came down he was waiting in the hall.

'Thanks for today, you worked really hard,' he said, and paid me. 'I've got an idea. I won't always be here on Saturdays, at least not when you arrive, between weddings and other things I have to do. You can take these spare keys and let yourself in and I'll leave a note telling you what needs to be done. How's that?'

'Well, yes, if you're sure.'

'Of course I'm sure. I know you'll be okay,' he said, patting me on the back.

He showed me how to get past the triple lock on the inside door and I headed for home.

Now I knew it was not all in my head. That had been real. No doubt about it. I'd felt his hand down there. I know I didn't see it but I knew it was there. And I had keys to his house. Me, an altar boy, with keys to one of the priests' house. Not even the parish priest would have keys to Father Payne's house. I was a fairly senior altar boy but still just an altar boy. Some of the older altar boys had left. Now they were in the folk group. Father Payne's folk group. One of them was Simon (not his real name). He was very friendly with Father Payne. Some people said he even got to drive the new Renault 12 and he couldn't have been more than fourteen. Kevin (not his real name) used to be in the altar boys and he was in the folk group too. I cycled up to the gates at home. My mother asked what I'd been doing. I told her about the garden and the keys and nothing else.

On Sunday I told Terry I was leaving the altar boys. He was

disappointed but not surprised – I was twelve and interested in the folk group.

'I'll be sorry to see you leave. You and Stephen were always here, and you could always be relied upon.'

'Well, I'll still be around if you need any help setting up the altar or anything like that. And if you need any help with weddings you can just ask me.'

'I suppose you'll be joining the folk group.'

'Well, I'm thinking about it.'

'Playing the guitar and singing,' Terry said, laughing.

'Well, I can't play the guitar but we'll see.'

I was sad at leaving the altar boys – I had been there for a few years – but I wanted to do what the others were doing. I left Terry my surplice and soutane in case one of the new altar boys wanted to use it and walked home with my hands in my pockets.

Marion Grehan was twenty-two or -three and worked a lot in the sacristy. She helped the priests with letters and collection envelopes going out to the parish. There was also a small shop in the sacristy selling Mass cards, Rosary beads and statues, and Marion was always there. Father Finn had started a parish newsletter, *Cabra Parish News*, and Marion's name was at the bottom of nearly every article. I wanted to be in on all of this. I decided to write an article on the recent talent show in the parish hall. I wrote it out twice to make sure my handwriting was as good as I could get it. Marion was always in the sacristy on Monday evening and I walked round with my work. She was sitting in the parish office inside the sacristy. The room was full of files and boxes of envelopes. On the maps on the wall the parish was divided into three and shaded in different colours to show which parts each priest had to look after – Father Finn's in blue, Father Dooley's in red and the parish priest's in green.

Father Payne had a special job somewhere else so he didn't have an area to look after.

'Marion, can I come round here and help you in the parish office during the week?' I said.

'Yeah, sure, Andrew. There's always lots to be done – but don't you have homework to do? I don't want you getting into any trouble.'

'Well, I'd have to do my homework first, but after that couldn't I come round and help out?' I didn't want to be left out of what was going on in the church and Marion was involved with everything. She said I could come round whenever I wanted. And my article would be in the next parish newsletter. I went home happy.

Between then and Christmas I followed Marion everywhere. There was lots to do in the office. Boxes of envelopes to be sent to each house in the parish for weekly collections and Christmas donations. Articles to be written for the newsletter. Marion still wrote most of them but I went along when she interviewed people.

'Now, who was that?'

'That's Mr Brett,' she said, 'he's working with Father Finn on a plan to raise lots of money to help do the church up.'

'Aren't the Bretts in the folk group – the two girls, Sandra and the other one, Orlagh, the one my brother likes?'

'Yes, they're in the folk group.'

'I was thinking of joining the folk group.'

'That'd be great for you – seeing as you're not in the altar boys any more.'

There was a knock on the door at home. Stephen was upstairs doing his homework, Audrey and I were sitting watching television and my mother was in the kitchen.

'Mammy, Mammy, Father Payne is here.' She came through

to shake hands with our special guest. He took off his raincoat. He wore grey trousers, a black cardigan with a knitted belt, his collar and those funny high-heeled shoes that I'd heard the altar boys laugh about. He sat down with a big smile on his face.

I felt nervous but safe. I knew nothing was going to happen tonight. I liked the way he was dressed casually and at the same time you could still see he was a priest. His hair had just been washed and had that full look. The television was quickly turned off and Audrey and I were sent out to the kitchen to make tea and put some biscuits out on a plate.

'You know what cups to use,' my mother said, 'and bring in the milk and sugar.'

Father Payne had an armchair to himself. My mother had the other one and Audrey and I sat on the couch. We talked about school and homework, answering his questions politely. He knew my parents had split up and didn't bring up the subject. Although I knew I was safe I still felt very uncomfortable. When he looked at me I thought he could see right through me. I almost felt embarrassed and couldn't understand why. I went to the bathroom to get away from the room for a few minutes. 'He's the one who should be embarrassed,' I said to myself. In one way it *was* nice to have a priest in the house – Father Payne's special job was working in an office at the Archbishop's House so that made him even more important – but at the same time I couldn't wait for him to go home. After what he had done he could just pop into our house, and that frightened me. He was totally in control and I felt unable to do anything.

'So do you miss being in the altar boys?' he said when I came back into the room.

'Well, I've been busy doing other things – helping Marion in the parish office on Mondays and sometimes other days as well if she's busy, and Terry has asked me to help him out a few times.'

'What about the folk group, would you be interested and would you have time?'

Audrey and Stephen were already in the folk group. I knew they practised on Wednesday nights in a room just off the altar for about an hour, sometimes more. The folk group sang at the twelve o'clock Mass every Sunday morning. This was Father Payne's Mass. Since I'd left the altar boys it was the Mass I went to. Even when I was in the altar boys, I served whatever Mass I had to, then came back for the folk Mass. The church was always packed. Father Payne and his Mass were very popular – especially with young people. I'd heard people ask if he was part of the Charismatic Movement. I hoped not. As far as I knew that was for people who were a bit strange – standing around in groups holding hands and speaking in tongues. That wasn't what the Church was about at all.

'Well, I was thinking about it,' I said. I wanted to be back on the altar. I wanted to be seen on the altar. I didn't want to be part of the congregation, just watching. I wanted to be involved. 'I'm not sure if I'd be any good,' I said, feeling embarrassed again.

'Sure you know you can sing,' my mother said. It was true.

'Why don't you sing something for me now?' said Father Payne, which made me even worse. He was looking very relaxed and comfortable in his armchair and I could see he wasn't rushing anywhere.

I sang. 'Whatsoever You Do for the Likes of Your Brother, That You Do Unto Me' suddenly felt very long. When I finished Father Payne said I had a really nice voice and I agreed that I would join the folk group the following Wednesday.

Early in the New Year Terry and Father Finn said that I could take over running the altar boys. We had an altar boys' meeting nearly every week and it was now my job to do the rota for all the Masses. I started training new altar boys and took some of the other boys through practice sessions to make sure they were doing everything right. Between the altar boys, the folk group and helping Marion and Terry I was now spending a lot of time around the church. I was thirteen and already I knew all I wanted was to be a priest. After school I couldn't wait to finish my homework and go round to the church. If there was nothing going on there I just stayed at home and watched television.

Father Payne was still doing the same thing every Saturday afternoon and still I couldn't think of telling anyone. As the months went on he became more comfortable with what he was doing. He wasn't as careful or slow as he used to be. Sometimes he opened my trousers, pulled my underpants to one side and messed with me for ages. Other days he pulled my trousers and underpants down to my knees or ankles and sat me on his lap, or laid me across his lap, front up, while he messed around. I couldn't even think of talking to him about what he was doing. I didn't want to do anything that drew any attention to what was happening. All the time he was messing with me I never once looked down at what he was actually doing. I could just feel it all the time. I used the television as a way of pretending nothing was happening or just talked about something else – how things were at home or school. Once I started to get turned on by what he was doing. I was embarrassed. Time seemed to have stopped: I thought the horror of being there with him would never end. It was his first time to say anything.

'Are you getting excited?' he asked, without looking at me.

'No,' I said, as if I didn't even know what he meant.

From then on I concentrated on the television even more

so it wouldn't happen again. Whatever else was going on I was just watching television.

During the week there were times when I could tell myself that nothing at all was happening to me. But on Saturdays as we sat down on the couch, I felt myself panicking. I felt hot. I wanted to run out of the room or just start crying – anything to avoid what I knew would happen – but I was just too afraid. I never thought he would hit me or anything like that; I was just afraid to talk about it. Mostly I just sat or lay there, hating what he was doing and waiting for him to finish. As I cycled home my body would start to relax again. At home I could have a bath without anyone thinking it was strange: it was Saturday night and I was dirty and sometimes sweaty from a day spent in the garden. It would be a week before I had to go through it all again. In the meantime Father Payne would be the popular charismatic chaplain and it was only me who knew he was like two different people. And I could hide that – even from myself.

I liked everyone knowing that I worked in his house on Saturdays. It made me feel important to know that people in the church thought of me as his friend. He was a special priest and the church was the main part of my life. I didn't want to lose my important job. Although I hated what he was doing he made up for it in other ways. He allowed me to be seen with him. If I didn't cycle to his house he always gave me a lift home and people would see me in his car. Walking around the church grounds on Sunday mornings where everyone could see us felt great. I couldn't stop going to his house anyway. People would ask why. Had something gone wrong? Had *I* done something wrong? I could never cope with so many people asking questions when I knew what the answer was. If I just didn't turn up at the house I would still meet him in the church and he would want to know where I'd been. He might even call at the house again to see if I was okay. Was I sick or had I had an accident? Stopping what was going on meant having to face it. The best I could do was pretend it wasn't happening.

## 3. A Great Priest

During the following summer holidays Father Payne said we should take a day off from gardening.

'Would you like to come for a game of squash?' he asked as I arrived at his house.

'Well, em, when are you going?'

'We can go now. I have a court booked down at Clonliffe. Don't you have any sports gear from school? All you need is shorts and a tee-shirt. We can pick them up from your house on the way.'

I barely had time to think. I couldn't play squash so I'd probably end up looking stupid. I was never any good at school sports. Basketball, football or swimming – I was terrible at everything. The only sport I didn't hate was running because I didn't always come last.

Did they have showers? When I was much younger and had to go swimming in our local pool I always kept my shorts on in the shower. Lots of others did the same. Could I get out of having a shower in Clonliffe? I could feel myself panicking again.

'Well, you know, I've never played before so I wouldn't be any good.'

'It doesn't matter, it's only for the exercise.'

I knew I had no choice: I could never say no when he asked me to do something. I cycled home and picked up the sports gear I used in school. Father Payne arrived at the house a couple of minutes later and drove us to Drumcondra.

He picked up the keys from the front desk at Clonliffe

College. The huge grey building looked impressive from the outside. When I was old enough this would be my home for seven years and I would learn everything I needed to know to be a priest. The squash courts were between the college and the Archbishop's House. We let ourselves into the changing-rooms and Father Payne locked the door behind us in case anyone went through our bags while we were playing. That was the last thing I would have thought of in Clonliffe. If anyone else wanted to play squash they had to knock loudly on the door. We played the game. Father Payne showed me where to stand and where to aim the ball. I wasn't as bad as I thought I'd be and he didn't bother to keep the score, which helped.

'I think we've had enough now – what do you think?' he asked after nearly an hour.

'Okay.'

We headed for the changing-rooms.

'Did you bring a towel for after your shower?'

'No, I didn't bother. Sure I can have a bath when I get home.'

'I've brought extra towels so you might as well have a shower here. You'll only be standing around waiting for me anyway,' he said, getting undressed.

Apart from embarrassment I couldn't think of any excuse not to have a shower. I felt I had to. He waited until I was undressed, then we walked into the shower room. It had about seven large cubicles, all tiled. I did my best not to look at him naked. I didn't want him to think I was interested in some way. I wanted to finish as quickly as I could. That way I could start drying myself and maybe even get some clothes on before he was finished. He called me into his cubicle and told me to rub some soap all over his back. I started to do it but I was barely touching him. He told me to rub harder and then told me to go lower. I could tell by his voice that he was getting annoyed that I wouldn't rub him the way he wanted. I just carried on pretending that I thought I was doing it right. I was relieved when he said, 'Okay, that's enough,' and drove me home.

The following Saturday was even worse. We finished work earlier than usual and after I'd washed my hands in the bathroom he called me into his bedroom. I had been in his room loads of times before. If the weather was bad, like it was that day, I did cleaning and hoovering around the house. He was lying on the bed and told me to take off my shoes and lie down beside him. The room was dull. The curtains were only half-opened. A big, dark, heavy-looking wardrobe covered most of one wall. I did what I was told. He undid my trousers quickly and told me to lift myself up. When I did, he pulled off my trousers and underpants and put them on the floor beside the bed. He then took off his own trousers and baggy white underpants and lay back on the bed beside me. He put one arm around my shoulder and used his other hand to mess with me again. He looked at me from time to time but I just kept looking at the ceiling or towards the window.

'Now you do the same thing to me,' he said in a low voice.

I felt panicky and hot and my heart beat really fast. He put his hand on my right hand and put it near his genitals.

'Go on – there's nothing to be afraid of.'

He placed my hand on his genitals and then reached over to mess with me again. I could feel my hands were sweaty. My hand on his genitals didn't move. My eyes stared out the window. He messed with me for a while longer. I think he could see from looking at my face that I hated everything that was happening.

'Okay, I think we'll get dressed now,' he said at long last.

He passed me my clothes and I got dressed. Still shocked, I

was just glad it was over. Now Father Payne could go back to being the priest I admired and looked up to.

'Shall we go for a drive?' he asked as we walked back downstairs.

'Oh yeah, that'd be great.' I loved being in the car. And out of the house.

We drove to Dollymount beach, stopping for a burger and chips on the way. I knew I shouldn't have been eating so soon before my dinner but this was a treat. Father Payne drove far down the beach.

'Have you ever driven a car before?'

'Not properly. When my father drove us to school a few years ago he used to go in through the back of the fire station in Dorset Street where he worked. Whoever was sitting in the front seat of the car beside him got to steer the car into the station car park while he drove it really slowly. But that's about it.' I knew what he was going to say and I couldn't wait.

'Okay, I'll let you drive for a bit. Do you think you'll be able to manage that?'

'Well, it's automatic, isn't it? So I should be all right.' I tried not to let him see how excited I was in case he changed his mind. He might think he'd made a mistake.

'I'll get out of the car and go around to your side, you just jump across the seat. I don't want people to notice you,' he said.

I sat in the driver's seat and held on to the large steering wheel. Father Payne made sure I knew which was the accelerator and which was the brake. Then I drove. It felt great. The beach was not busy but there were enough cars and people around for me to have to use the brake to slow down and then speed up again as if I was driving out on the street. After a while I turned the car around and drove back up the beach and then back down again.

'Okay, I think that's enough for now, pull in anywhere and we'll head back,' he said. His hand was on my knee. I'd had a great time. If only people from Cabra had seen me driving his car.

I sang with the folk group and watched Father Payne come out to say Mass.

'Good morning, everyone.'

'Good morning, Father.'

'You're all very welcome to this morning's celebration of Mass.'

He was totally in control and everyone looked up to him as he celebrated Mass. If only they knew, I thought to myself. Sometimes he came out on to the altar before Mass and tried to get the parishioners to practise the folk songs. None of the other priests did anything like that. He encouraged me to sing solo in front of a packed church. When we rehearsed on Wednesday evenings he could see I was nervous but always told me I could do it. His sermons were always interesting. When he said Mass it was as if he was talking to the people every week about something new and not just reading out the same thing every Sunday. He turned the confession box into a confessional room. I had a look one Saturday evening when he wasn't around. The small dark room where you knelt down was gone. There was a small room with a table, a lamp and two chairs. You just sat down and told Father Payne your sins face to face. None of the other priests got involved. When I wanted to go to confession I went to St Peter's in Phibsboro. The priests in Cabra knew me too well. I didn't go very often. I never really felt I'd done anything wrong. Saturday afternoons were not my fault; Father Payne was the one doing things. I felt guilty because I wanted to be a priest. That meant I should not have been involved in anything like this. I felt guilty too because I liked him so much, because I enjoyed the attention that he gave me – keys to his house, lifts in his car. But then I couldn't get out of it. I felt bad that I wasn't able to say no. That made me feel helpless.

At school I watched the other fellas in class. There was no way they would have let Father Payne do this to them, so looking at them made me feel worse. I knew I was different, wanting to be a priest, but I didn't mind that. They didn't seem to mind either. Others got picked on in ways I never did. Paul Ward got a few clatters because he wasn't liked all that much and fellas thought he wouldn't fight back. Nobody could stand Noel Kelly because he was such a snob; even teachers picked on him sometimes. I walked to and from school with Tony McCauley who lived near us on Attractta Road. In class Tommy O'Neill and Michael Gunn were friends and they were a good laugh. But even though I had friends, Father Payne made me feel different from them in a way I didn't like. I wondered if he was doing the same thing to Simon. I couldn't imagine it: Simon was good-looking – taller and older-looking than me. But he and Father Payne did spend a lot of time together during the week. Father Payne's car was always outside his house. Maybe he just got on well with the family. He hadn't been back to our house since before last Christmas and, although he was important, I wasn't sorry.

Father Payne never took me back to his bedroom except to clean. Even when I was only nine or ten I was always good at cleaning, hoovering and washing up after dinner at home. I always liked to leave the area around the sink in such a way that you could see how clean and tidy it was the minute you walked into the kitchen. Almost as if it hadn't even been used. I was the same in the garden. I cut the grass tight and made sharp borders between the edge of the grass and the black clay so that they both stood out. When I was in the Cubs I tried to wear white knee-length socks because I liked the way they showed up my polished black shoes and dark navy short trousers. I cleaned Father Payne's house well and he paid me. Now he kept his interfering to messing around on the couch. He never uncovered himself again. And he never again asked me to do anything to him.

I always enjoyed the run-up to Christmas. Practising carols with the folk group weeks in advance meant it all started early. I sang solo more often now. It made me a bit nervous but I still wanted to do it. And I loved when it went well. This year it also meant getting to know our new parish priest, Father Moroney. He was a tall man, well into his fifties, bald with some white hair around the back of his head, and he wore his black suit and collar all the time. Word had it that he didn't like the folk group: he didn't like us young people on the altar and he didn't like the guitars or our songs. He drove a very old Morris Minor. Meanwhile, Father Payne had bought a brand-new Toyota Carina. After practice one night we all went out to have a look. I loved it. He sat in, gave us a wave and drove Simon home. Although I was the one he liked to mess with, Simon was closer to him and I didn't like it. I was the one going to be a priest and though Father Payne was a great priest he didn't seem to care about this. Seeing how much he liked Simon, I was jealous. Simon didn't have to put up with everything I did.

It was busy around in the sacristy. The repository, as the shop was now called, was so popular that everyone wondered how they ever managed without it. People could come in and buy Mass cards and pay to have masses said for the dead. There were Rosary beads and religious books and at Christmas, candles and cribs. Of course, once it was set up Marion was left to do most of the work, but I was happy to help. Being Christmas, there was lots to do at home as well, and I was glad to be on holiday from school. But working round at the church always came first. Every Sunday morning I went round to the sacristy at about half past nine. I stayed with Marion in the repository and helped serve customers. The men who collected the baskets during the two church collections stayed in the same room though there were different collectors for each Mass. Terry was there as well, helping to count the money when he wasn't busy looking after the priests and the altar. And then, when each Mass was ready to start, this was the room the priest and the altar boys passed through to go out on to the altar. There was a small round peephole so we could see out on to the altar and down as far as the first few rows of people in the congregation. When the priests came through the room people stopped talking to one another and said hello and good morning to them. When Father Moroney came through everyone stayed quiet. Sometimes he called Terry to one side to complain that he could smell cigarette smoke and told him to have a word with the collectors. Every week I got to see everything that had to be done in the church on a busy Sunday morning. I loved it. I wanted to spend some time in the priests' room but knew I wouldn't be allowed. They needed to be able to talk privately but I wanted to be part of it. I couldn't wait till I was.

After the eleven o'clock Mass Terry cleared the altar and started to get it ready for the folk Mass. It was my job to put out all the extra microphones for the folk group and check they all worked. Lorraine, Oonagh, Vera and some of the others in the group put leaflets on the church seats with the words of the songs. We all prepared for what felt like the Mass of the week. The church filled up quickly. As far as I could see, the same people sat near the front of the church and in the same seats every week. If people came into the church late they'd be lucky to find a seat and usually they had to stand. We generally sang two songs during Holy Communion. In between these Father Payne used to give us Communion, which meant the people at the altar had to wait. One morning he put some hosts on the small gold paten that usually covered the chalice and handed it to Vincent, who was one of the singers.

'Would you like to give Communion to the folk group please, Vincent?' said Father Payne. Vincent looked shocked as the paten was put into his hands. We gathered around him in a circle as he gave us Communion. Some of us giggled. Some of the older ones did not look happy at what had happened. On one hand I was impressed that Father Payne was being so trendy: old rules didn't seem to matter; the important thing was that we all came to Mass and we all received Communion. On the other hand, if he was to choose someone other than a priest to give out Communion he should have chosen the next best thing – me. Vincent got to give out Communion many times before Father Payne changed his mind and started doing it himself again. After Mass I helped clear off the altar and went out to the side doors of the church where the rest of the folk group hung around for a while talking before we all went home.

In January I went back to school to finish second year. I felt very uncomfortable in class. I always had my homework done and didn't get into trouble but I felt so different to everyone around me. Outside school my life seemed miles removed from theirs. They talked about football and basketball. Mr Hartigan, the basketball coach, tried to get me to play to see if I was any good but I was useless. Everyone else seemed so confident and able. At school I had no way of covering up for myself. In Cabra people knew me as the fella who was always around in the church. As Father Payne's friend. As Marion's helper. As Terry's assistant. I had loads to hide behind. At school I had nothing.

I felt I looked as different as I knew I was. I got on with people but I wasn't one of them. There was something about me that was wrong. I knew what it was but tried not to think about it. Though it had been going on now for nearly two years, still there were days when I could hardly believe it was really happening. And it was there every day. The thoughts would just come out of nowhere. Between classes someone would start talking about meeting girls after school at the convent and it hit me how different that was from meeting Father Payne at the weekend. During a biology lesson one day Mr Horgan asked what we wanted to know about the human body 'in terms of reproduction'.

'Girls,' said one fella. 'I want to know more about girls and their bodies, and how they work, that sort of thing.' If they knew how much Father Payne knew about my body they'd be shocked. And here they were asking teachers about the facts of life. Father Payne had already asked me ages ago if I knew much about the facts of life. I told him no as we sat on the couch with my trousers open and his hands all over me. I was afraid that if I said yes he'd ask me to tell him what I knew. The following week he showed me a book with pictures and diagrams. He did all the talking and I didn't ask any questions. Afterwards he carried on as he usually did. I knew enough by then to know that he was probably just trying to get me excited again by talking about sex. It didn't work. Mr Horgan told us all about girls and Father Payne went to the back of my mind.

Later that year the Pope came to Ireland. The houses in Cabra were all decorated with yellow and white flags. Some people even put his picture in their front window. Father Finn had asked me weeks earlier to bring the altar boys to the Phoenix Park for the Mass. At first I thought we were going to serve the Mass but as the day came nearer it turned out he just wanted us there as part of the congregation. Still, I was really happy. There were too many altar boys for me to look after up in the park so Marion agreed to come with me. Like everyone else, she was going to the Mass anyway. We met the altar boys outside the gates of the church at about half-five that morning. There were already loads of people in the streets heading towards the park. Everything felt really special. I was so excited at the thought of seeing the Pope. I wondered how near we would be to him. Would I get to shake hands with him?

When we took our places in the park I realized we'd be lucky if we even got to see him. And it was hours later before he arrived but it was worth it. Everyone was waving flags, clapping and singing. After the Mass when he went around in his 'Popemobile' we got a much better view of him and then we all went home. That night I went round to Marion's house to watch the whole thing again on television and got to see everything we couldn't see during the day.

Two days later, on the Sunday night, a rumour spread that the Pope would be passing through the parish on his way up to the Papal Nuncio's house on the Navan Road. It was hard to believe at first, but lots of people were coming out on to the street so it looked like something was happening. Audrey and I went over to the roundabout across from our house and met Marion and some of the others from the folk group. All of our neighbours were out as well. After only a short while both sides of the street were full of people for as far as we could see in both directions. Everyone talked about their day in the park. How near they were to the altar. How far away. How long the queues for the toilet were. None of us could believe that the Pope would be in Cabra, that we were getting an extra chance to see him. I saw Father Payne on the far side of the road smiling and chatting to everyone. I felt sad seeing him. It sort of spoiled the night. Every now and then a police car or a Guard on a motor-bike came over the bridge at the far end of Faussaugh Road and everyone cheered before realizing it was a false alarm. Then there were lots of lights. The whole bridge area was lit up with bright headlights and flashing blue beacons. The Pope had arrived in Cabra. We cheered loudly and waved as the cars came nearer. How would I know which one he was in? And then I saw him and waved like mad. This was much closer than in the park. It was all over in seconds but it was a great night.

# 4. Moving On

School was becoming harder. Exams were looming. I was now in third year and knew I had to do my Inter Cert the following summer. I did all my homework. There were some nights when it took hours to do. But I still did very little studying. I was okay when I had things that kept me busy – actual pieces of work like essays or French translation – but just reading or studying was difficult. I couldn't concentrate. When I was much younger I loved reading. I'd read all Enid Blyton's *Famous Five* books and even some of Alfred Hitchcock's collections of detective stories. But studying meant being alone in the bedroom with my books and I didn't like it. If it was a night when there was something to be done in the church that's where I wanted to be. I started my homework after school and finished it when I came back from the church.

Over the next few months Father Payne continued to interfere with me. In the early months of 1980 he didn't open my trousers as fully as he used to – just enough to get his hand inside my underpants and rest it there or mess around a little bit. With my mock exams coming up I saw my chance to stop going to his house. I had tried once before about a year and a half earlier when I was still only thirteen. I had told him that as it was coming into the autumn there was no need for me to come down every week to do gardening. He told me to keep coming down because even if the weather was bad he'd find something for me to do in the house.

Now, even though I was nervous and didn't want to get

embarrassed, things had changed. There had been the Saturday recently when he'd shouted at me, calling me an idiot because he thought I'd taken a telephone message wrongly. After all he'd done to me he was calling me an idiot over nothing. He apologized but there was something about it that made me really angry. I was sure he'd never call Simon an idiot.

There was worse than that. One night in the middle of an altar boys' meeting Father Payne walked into the room off the altar.

'Hi, everyone,' he said, with a beaming smile. 'How are you all?'

The altar boys, about fifteen of them, were all very pleased to see him. Who wouldn't be, I thought to myself.

'Can I just interrupt your meeting, Andrew? I have one or two things to announce.'

He stood beside me facing the altar boys.

'At a meeting of the priests of the parish we have decided that I should help out with training and looking after the altar boys.'

The smile was gone and he looked serious. I felt myself getting angry and embarrassed.

'So I think the best thing to do is divide into two groups depending on age. How many of you are under ten? And under twelve? And under fourteen?'

Father Payne decided to take the over-twelves and said I should look after the rest. I couldn't believe what was happening. This was *my* altar boys' meeting. Why had he not talked to me about this first? I thought I must have looked really stupid in front of everyone.

'Is that okay with you, Andrew?' he asked.

He knew me well enough by then to know I wasn't going to say no. Especially in front of everyone else. He carried on talking. I had to get out of the room.

'I'll be back in a minute – there's just something I have to do,' I said.

Marion was in the parish office and I told her what had just happened. I was upset and angry. Working at the church was everything to me and I didn't like Father Payne treating me so casually.

'Well, if he wants to look after the altar boys he can look after all of them – I'm not having anything to do with it any more.' I tore up the rota I had prepared for the following Sunday Masses and threw it in the bin.

Marion agreed that we could leave the sacristy early and invited me round to her house for a cup of tea. I didn't want to be there when Father Payne finished *his* altar boys' meeting. A few days later I met him in the sacristy and told him I didn't want to be involved with the altar boys.

'Okay, if that's what you want,' he said, sounding annoyed. He didn't smile and left without saying goodbye.

I used my exams as an excuse not to come to his house any more.

'I've got my mock exams coming up soon so I'll have to spend more time studying at the weekends. It means that I won't be able to come down on Saturday for a while.'

I didn't want to say it was for good. If I sounded too definite he might start asking questions. Better to be as casual as possible. He didn't seem surprised. He knew I was fifteen years old and about to do my Inter. I was old enough to get away from him. He didn't seem upset in any way.

'I'm sure I'll still see you around at the church. What about the folk group? Will you have time for that or do you think you should cut that out too?'

'I'll be okay for the moment and just see how it goes.'

I felt like a part of my life was coming to an end. I knew Father Payne would probably never touch me again and I was glad it was over. But did this mean I wasn't special any more? That I wouldn't be his friend? I was confused and very sad.

I sat my exams and then worried all through the summer because I knew how little I had studied. I spent Sunday mornings in the sacristy and continued singing with the folk group for a few months before I left it. I started to see Father Payne in a different light. Once he was a role model. Now he was the opposite.

I had started to wear dark clothes. Whenever my mother was buying me clothes I persuaded her to get me something navy or black. Better still was when she gave me the money and I could go and buy something myself. There wasn't much to start with – dark grey trousers for going back to Declan's that September instead of light grey. All I needed was a dark jumper or a shirt and I would start to look the part – certainly more priestly than Father Payne. So often did he remove his collar when he came off the altar that now he was hardly ever dressed as a priest. Other times he turned up on Sunday mornings with a light grey suit and his black collar, looking very sophisticated; some people said distinguished. I never saw him in a black suit. His casual appearance was something I used to like about him, but not any more. It seemed like he didn't take the priesthood seriously.

I never saw him train the altar boys. But he did take groups of them for drives in his car and to McDonald's for the occasional treat. We still chatted in the sacristy and in some way I felt we were on more level terms. He had no control over me now and I would show him who was the real priest. I even joked with him one morning that some of us liked to say the Creed, because he had started to leave it out of the Mass. Then I sat in the congregation and as he asked people to stand for the Creed he grinned down at me and I smiled back. On a rare Monday evening when he did the Benediction I was disappointed when I heard him say to Father Dooley, 'I'm not going to bother with the Rosary, they can say that themselves.' I still went to his Mass but could not take him seriously as a priest any more. And yet I could see how popular he was. His Sunday Mass was packed. Even I couldn't stay away. Everyone still loved him. But I knew it wasn't for real.

I went back to Declan's. My dark trousers didn't get me into too much trouble but the four honours and four passes I got in my Inter did. Teachers were waiting in the corridors to tell us which class we were to go into. Having spent three years in the A class I was now told to go into the C class. Four honours looked good at home but compared to some of the other fellas' results it wasn't good at all. Most of my classmates were staying in either the A or the B class and I hardly knew anyone in the C class. I felt sick.

Mr O'Malley took us for our first class. I'd had him for religion a year earlier so he knew me already. He sat on one of the desks and looked around at his new students.

'Well, Andrew, the tables would appear to have turned – what happened?' he said.

There was a horrible silence in the room.

'I don't know,' I muttered finally.

Just then the door opened and Mr McCormack walked in. He was the school manager, whom we nicknamed Barney.

'Excuse me, Mr O'Malley, it looks like we're a few lads short in the B class, I just want to look around and see if we've anyone suitable to go in there.'

He walked around the class and picked four of us. I never felt so lucky in all my life. I couldn't have been happier walking into the room next door. Mr Duggan was taking the class and told us to take seats wherever we could. I sat in the front row beside Brendan Foster. Mr Duggan came over and said it was really nice to have me in his class. He knew me to talk to and he had known my brother for years. With everyone else talking no one heard what he said apart from Brendan.

Our teachers for fifth year told us that compared to what lay ahead of us the Inter had been a doddle. Just because we had done well didn't mean we could take it easy. We had to work very hard for the next two years. Most of the teachers were okay. Our English and history teacher was sarcastic, but the sarcasm only worked because we were not allowed to answer back. At first it looked like fifth year might turn out to be all right.

A few weeks before Christmas I was watching the news at home and saw the awful effects of a huge earthquake in Italy. The Pope had gone to the scene to see for himself the damage that had been done – houses ruined, villages destroyed and thousands of people homeless having lost everything. The Irish Red Cross launched an appeal for donations and I wondered if there was anything I should do. What could one schoolboy do on his own? What difference would it make so far away? I thought about getting people in the parish to donate money to give to the Irish Red Cross. How could I organize this? If I went to the priests they would probably take over. Or, more likely, they might not like the idea – preferring only to ask the people for money when it was coming directly into the church or the parish. This was something I would have to start myself and show that I could do it. And I wanted people to see me doing it, although I would need Marion's help: she was a great organizer. We planned to get about twenty people from the parish to take on one or two roads each. I wanted this to be a young people's project so we asked friends from the folk group, Tony McCauley from school, and some of Audrey and Stephen's friends. Marion and I got letters printed up for each house in the parish telling everyone what was happening and pointing out that this was a parish effort. The letters were delivered and each volunteer told the people on their road that they would be back in a few days to collect any donations. That gave people in the parish time to check out that everything was okay and they knew only to give their donations to the same person who had delivered the letter. Father Payne gave his full support. Father Moroney said nothing – apparently because we hadn't asked his permission. With so many young people doing good, I didn't think his permission was needed. But his approval would have been appreciated.

The collection went well. Envelopes flooded in and we raised nine hundred and forty-five pounds. I was delighted. A small idea at home had turned into a great success, all of it done by young people in the parish. Marion and I delivered a cheque over to the offices of the Irish Red Cross at Merrion Square. I was excited. I wondered what their reaction would be to so much money. A middle-aged lady at reception took the envelope and asked if we wanted a receipt or could we wait until they posted one out.

'Well, we can wait,' I replied.

'Okay then, thank you very much.'

Is that it? I thought to myself. No hand-shake. No tea and biscuits. No invitation to come in and sit down so they could tell us what the money might be used for.

Early in the New Year I got a letter from the General Secretary of the Irish Red Cross thanking me for sending on 'this very generous donation' on behalf of the people of Cabra and saying it was 'very much appreciated'. That was more like it. I was delighted that our hard work was being officially recognized. We could print the letter in the parish newsletter so people could see where their money had gone. And maybe they could see just what a good priest I would make. I was wearing black quite a lot now, mostly around the church but sometimes in school as well. I was sort of creating a second person for me to be. Showing a persona for the real me to hide behind. As time went by I began to believe it was working. It seemed that everyone who saw or knew me realized I wanted to be a priest and they never thought to look beyond that. That suited me because I didn't want to look there either. It was the same as me looking at Father Payne. I could see the popular priest that everyone else saw and that helped me block out the other Father Payne. And if I could block him out, then I could block out what he had done. At least sometimes.

Apart from Tony McCauley, who was part of the team, nobody in school knew about the money we raised for the Red Cross. I had told Broncho – Brother McLoughlin – at the school carol service and he told me I was great. I was pleased but embarrassed. 'I mean it,' he said, 'you really are great.' People in the streets around Cabra stopped Marion and me and told us we had done a great job. As soon as all the fuss died down I felt a bit lost. It was not a busy time in the parish office and I had no other jobs now. School was okay but there were times when I was very down about feeling so alone. I looked back on everything that had happened with Father Payne and wished I could have stopped it sooner. But I hadn't. It wasn't surprising I felt different. Looking around the classroom, I wondered who else would have let it start, never mind let it go on for nearly three years. But they hadn't been there, they wouldn't understand how someone like him could control you. I had been there and that made me different.

Some of them had girlfriends. I could never imagine myself with a girlfriend. I didn't want one: I was going to be a priest and I would never have sex. That didn't bother me either. I couldn't imagine anyone in class having sex. Not for a long time. I liked the look of certain people, both fellas and girls. I wondered what it would be like to be close to them as friends. It didn't worry me that I thought of some fellas as attractive because I never thought of that as sexual or as anything that was going to develop into anything physical. There was one guy in my class whom I liked more than the others. I really had a crush on him and thought he was extremely attractive in every way. I wanted so much to be better friends with him, but not in a sexual way. Not consciously anyway. Thinking about him added to my feelings of sadness and solitude. I was very down, and nervous and anxious just being around groups of people. As time passed I felt worse than when I had to go to Father Payne's every week.

## 5. A Secret Shared

I needed to talk to someone. I just wanted to talk about how bad I was feeling. Mr Duggan was a possibility; he was the only teacher I would have sat down and had a conversation with. There was a priest who came into the school occasionally from Cabra West, Father Martin O'Farrell. I thought about him, but I knew Mr Duggan much better. There was no way I was telling my parents. They would want to know why I was so depressed and would ask lots of questions – questions too embarrassing to answer. And I wasn't telling anyone in the church.

I went to see Mr Duggan, unsure of what I was going to say. As he was the guidance counsellor he was the only teacher with his own office, something the other teachers didn't like.

'Hi, Andrew, come in, take a seat.'

'Hello, Mr Duggan.'

He was also the only teacher who didn't have a nickname or who wasn't called by his surname when fellas were talking about him. Some people even called him Ken when they were talking to him but most of us still called him Mr Duggan. We chatted about school for a short while and then I started to tell him that I was having problems. All the time it was in the back of my mind to tell him about Father Payne. Will I or won't I? I could feel my heart beating faster and faster. I felt so sad I just started crying. Mr Duggan passed me over a box of tissues and told me everything would be okay.

'Well, there's something I have to tell you,' I said, still crying. 'I think you'll be a bit shocked.' I had already told him the year before that I wanted to be a priest. What would he think of me now?

'You can tell me anything. Don't worry — I won't be shocked. Just take your time.'

'It's about Father Payne, I think I told you about him before when we were talking about the priesthood. You said you knew him from years ago in Clonliffe.'

'Ivan Payne? Yes, I remember him.'

'Well, it's to do with him.' I could hardly believe what I was about to say. 'Emm.' I paused. 'He's been doing things to me, you know . . . he's been messing with my private parts.'

I had stopped crying. I was shocked at what I'd just done, too shocked even to cry. Mr Duggan looked more serious than I'd ever seen him look before. I thought he must be shocked too.

'Okay, Andrew, now I know how difficult this is but I need you to tell me exactly what has been happening. Is he still doing this?'

'No, it ended nearly a year ago.'

'Do you remember when it started?'

'Well, I can't be sure but it went on for a long time.'

'Well, when you say a long time would that be months or longer?' he asked, still serious but quiet and calm.

'Oh, much longer. It went on for years. I can hardly even remember it starting. It was before I came to Declan's so that's nearly four years ago.'

'So you would have been eleven or twelve then?'

'Yeah, around that.'

'I'm sorry, Andrew, but I need to know exactly what he's been doing. I know it's difficult, but I need to know.'

I didn't want to go into any detail but I knew that there was no getting out of it. I kept it very short. I told Mr Duggan what normally happened when I used to go to Father Payne's house. He was really shocked, especially because he knew Father Payne. He said I could get help to talk about what had happened. He even offered to arrange it but I didn't want to talk about it. All I really wanted to do was tell him that it had happened and tell him how sad I felt all the time. Just so I wasn't the only one to know. I didn't want to talk to anyone else about it. I cried and talked a bit more and Mr Duggan listened. Then he had an idea of his own.

'I think we'll have to tell someone about this. I don't want you to think you've told me something in private and I'm running out to tell everyone, so I'll tell you what I think we should do and you can tell me how you feel about it, how's that?'

'Well, I'm not telling my parents and I don't want anyone else telling them either,' I said, getting a bit worried.

'No, don't worry, I won't tell them if you don't want me to. And even if you do want me to tell them for you, I'll do that as well. Whatever you want, whatever helps you.'

I knew I could trust him.

'I can go and speak to someone I know in the church and tell them what you've said. Then they will speak to Father Payne and we'll just have to wait and see what he has to say.'

I thought he meant he was going to speak to one of the other priests in Cabra.

'No. I'll have to go to Archbishop's House in Drumcondra. There's a guy there I know, a priest, Alex Stenson. I'll speak to him and he'll do everything very quietly and carefully.'

I agreed that this was the right thing to do. He told me I could take some time to think about it but I said no. I was happy for him to go to Archbishop's House. I went back to my class and spent the rest of the day in a daze. What was going to happen to Father Payne? What would he say the next time he saw me? What if he said I was telling lies? Then someone might have to tell my parents that I had told some very serious lies about him. But I felt better that I had told someone.

Mr Duggan asked to see me the following day. I couldn't believe he'd have news for me so soon. It turned out he just wanted to make sure I was okay. I was glad he was on my side. The day before he explained that although the church would want to hear what Father Payne had to say he had no doubt that I was telling the truth. He knew my family well enough to know I wouldn't make up something like that.

Within a few days he told me that he had been to see Father Alex Stenson. Father Stenson had known Father Payne for years – they were in the same class at Clonliffe College and now they both worked at Archbishop's House. In fact, when he was talking to Father Stenson, Mr Duggan could hear Father Payne's voice in the next room. Father Stenson could not believe what he was being told and said he couldn't deal with my allegations. He told Mr Duggan that he would report what had been said to one of Dublin's bishops, Bishop Dermot O'Mahony. I'd heard of him. The Bishop would be talking to Father Payne and he would let Mr Duggan know what happened as soon as possible.

Because things had been so quiet at Christ The King, the only time people would notice I wasn't around was on Sunday mornings. There was no way I could go around to the sacristy as normal, not knowing whether the Bishop had spoken to Father Payne. In a way I didn't want to any more. By telling on Father Payne I'd cut myself off from everything at the church. Maybe the other priests in the parish would find out what had happened. Maybe everyone in the sacristy would know and would be talking about me. I could still call round to Marion's house. If anything was going on she'd be sure to tell me. But otherwise I would have to stay away. On Sunday morning I stayed at home. My mother asked why and I told her I wanted to go to the evening folk Mass in the church on the Navan Road. Like everyone else, she thought it was strange but I said I just wanted to see what it was like. Also the Navan Road church was where fellas from Declan's would be going to Mass and I might get to see some of them.

Our Lady Help of Christians on the Navan Road was as big a church as the one in Cabra. Apart from during Lent I was not used to going to Mass in the evening. But over the next few weeks I began to enjoy Mass in what I began to think of as my new parish. I saw fellas from school, some with their families or with other friends. The congregation was mixed but there were plenty of young people and I really enjoyed the folk group. The priests were older than the priests in Cabra and they all wore black. I got to know their different styles very quickly. The parish priest, Father Maher, gave good sermons most of the time. He seemed to be at his best when he was giving out about something – like young people taking drugs up at the corner of Baggott Road. He was about the same age as Father Moroney but he was more down to earth, more natural, not so holy. Father Kelly was a bit boring and forgot what he was talking about many times during sermons – which was usually the only interesting thing about them. Father Duffy was the priest I most wanted to see walking out on to the altar on Sunday evenings. He was in his late forties or early fifties, kept his white hair greased back and was almost always in black. His sermons were great and he said the Eucharist with a passion I planned to copy. The Navan Road church felt warm and genuine. I felt good there in a way that I hadn't for ages in Cabra. At the same time it felt strange being a member of the congregation. I didn't even know what the sacristy looked like.

*

Mr Duggan asked to see me again. It was a few weeks since he had been to Archbishop's House and I was surprised we'd heard nothing.

'Well, I was told that Bishop O'Mahony or someone in his office would get back to me, but they never did so eventually I contacted him myself.' He sounded annoyed. 'They've spoken to Father Payne and he has accepted that what you've said is true. Why they didn't get back to us with this information sooner I don't know. But the main thing is he's admitted it, so what we need to do is concentrate on you and make sure you're okay.'

'Well, I'm okay at the moment' – I didn't want to talk about it any more – 'but what's going to happen to Father Payne?'

'They say they're going to deal with him from here on. I didn't want to ask them what they were going to do to him: it would look like we just wanted to know the gory details about whether he would be punished and so on. As I say, they've told me they're going to deal with him.'

Mr Duggan said his door would always be open and I should stop by for a chat as often as I wanted.

I hadn't seen Father Payne for weeks. It felt longer. I saw his car in the distance once or twice but I hadn't actually come face to face with him yet. I'd been around to Marion's house a couple of times. I was sure that I would have been able to tell by her manner if she'd heard anything strange about me. Just like my family, Marion was surprised that I'd started going to another church. I told anyone who asked that I'd made new friends there who were my own age and I just liked going to that church. 'Oh, so we're not good enough for you any more,' some people said.

In fact I hadn't made any new friends at all, so I waited for Father Duffy one Friday evening after half-seven Mass. There was hardly anyone else left in the church and he could see me hanging around as he walked down the aisle.

'Hi, Father, my name is Andrew. Em, I wondered if I could just have a word with you?'

'Yeah, sure, do you want to come over to the house?' he replied in his strong country accent. I was delighted.

Father Duffy lived just across the road from the church and Father Kelly lived beside him. Father Maher lived in a huge house right beside the church.

He took me into the sitting-room at the back of the house.

'Well, Andrew, what's happening, are you just visiting us or have you moved into the parish or what?'

'Well, I live in Cabra, down on Quarry Road – I don't know if you know it – near the statue of Our Lady?'

'Yes, I know it. And who are you living with down there?'

'There's my mother, my sister and my brother, and my father lives near us. I'm in fifth year in Declan's and I was just wondering – you see, I've always wanted to be a priest and because of that I've spent a lot of time helping out in the church in Cabra and doing church things. I don't really have any friends my own age and I thought you might be able to introduce me to some young people.'

'Yes, I'm sure I could. Tell us, how long have you felt this way about the priesthood?' he asked.

'For as far back as I can remember. I've never wanted to be anything else. I've just always thought that the best way to live my life to the fullest would be as a priest. I like the church and I think the work priests do is really great. I know it means being on call to the parish nearly twenty-four hours a day but I still like it and I just can't wait to get to Clonliffe.'

Father Duffy said there was a 'nice young group' who ran the summer project and he was sure they would need some help when the project started in the early summer. He told me to leave it for a few weeks and then get back to him.

I walked home happy. I felt I had a happier future. Easter was not long over and I wished I didn't have to wait so long for the project. I really didn't have much to do. During the week I did homework and not much else. On Monday nights I went to the Rosary and Benediction on the Navan Road and then there was Mass on Friday, Saturday and Sunday evenings at half-seven. The run-up to Easter had been great with Mass every night but that was over and now I just had to wait about six or eight weeks for the summer.

One Saturday morning I decided to go around to Christ The King church. I wasn't sure why I was going. I didn't miss it, because I liked the Navan Road church so much, but I still wanted to see it one more time. Saturday morning meant there would be confessions. Father Payne might be there. It was a while now since I'd told on him, so maybe he wasn't around any more. Once the idea was in my head I had to go round.

I didn't see Father Payne's car outside but then Simon could have borrowed it. I stood just inside the side door which was half-way up the church. There were a few people there after ten o'clock Mass but it wasn't busy. Terry came out on to the altar and then went back into the sacristy a couple of times. Two ladies were busy getting flowers ready for Sunday morning. The church was as cold as it always was but it felt empty as well. There was no special feeling there any more. In fact there was no feeling at all. It was hard to imagine all the times that I'd felt so excited by being there. Serving Mass on a cold Christmas morning as everyone sang carols really loudly and Miss Curran boomed out music on the organ. Rehearsing for all the extra services that made Easter such a busy time. Then there was the day when Archbishop Ryan came to do the confirmations. His driver had been talking to me in the sacristy and I told him I was going to be a priest. He told the Archbishop who came out of the priests' room and shook hands with me. Afterwards I couldn't remember what questions he'd asked me or what I'd said back to him but it felt great. Then there were nerves on days when I had to sing solo in the folk group but that felt good too. And now there was nothing. I didn't even feel sad. I looked around the church and wondered how I'd stayed so long. How could it all have meant so much for so long and now nothing? I couldn't understand.

Father Payne came from my left and passed by me going towards the door.

'Hi, Andrew, how are you?' He half smiled.

'I'm fine, thanks.' And he was gone.

I couldn't believe I'd found the words to answer him. And why wasn't he angry with me? There were people around but he was even friendly. Of course he didn't stop and chat, which he would have done before, so I knew he definitely had been questioned by Bishop O'Mahony as we had been told. I waited for a while to give him time to leave. Would he be waiting outside? Maybe someone had stopped him and they would be outside talking and I'd have to walk past them. The thought of it embarrassed me. I walked out of the church. He was gone and I hurried home.

Summer came and I was glad to get out of Declan's for a while. Mr Wall had spoken to my father about my grades and said I was capable of much more than I was doing. I'd promised to work harder in sixth year and tried to forget about it for the summer. I knew I needed the Leaving Cert to get into Clonliffe but studying was difficult. Concentrating was impossible.

I was nervous going up to the summer project on the first

night. I didn't know what I'd have to do. Or who would be there. Would they like me? How many fellas from school would be there – most fellas going to Declan's were from the Navan Road, not Cabra, so there was bound to be some. Father Duffy introduced me to some of the leaders. Some people were on holidays from school and others were already working so they would only be coming to the project at night. We were standing outside the parish centre at the back of the church, gathered around a leader's car. There were lots of new faces and names to remember – Val, Trisha, Maeve, Edel, Brian, Declan, Damien, Liam, Janet and loads more. Everyone was friendly. Edel gave me a huge hug and they all cheered. Janet did the same and I felt great. Inside the project grounds there were all sorts of sports and games going on but a lot of the leaders were standing out at Liam's car laughing and joking. I joined in the laughing but didn't say too much. Everyone knew everyone else and I had the whole summer ahead of me to get to know people. Now I just enjoyed being one of the gang.

When the project finished at ten o'clock we all headed for the chipper on Kinvara Avenue about ten minutes' walk away. This had become the done thing after the previous year's project. We had our burgers and chips sitting on the wall of someone's house opposite the chipper and afterwards walked around the parish as one by one people reached their houses. First Edel on Park Road and then Maeve a few doors down. Then Helen on the corner of Kinvara and Trisha a bit further up. Everyone got goodnight hugs. Then Brian, Declan and I walked back down the Navan Road. They took a right at Skreen Road and I carried on home.

The project was open at ten o'clock every morning during the week and closed at five. It re-opened from seven till ten for the over-fourteens. We had basketball, volleyball, tennis and football leagues. During the first few weeks I had to referee the under-fourteen matches during the day although I hadn't a clue about football. Luckily most people watched the volleyball leagues so I got away with it. And I told the teams that playing off-side was a bad idea because 'not enough people understand it'. That seemed to fool them and it made it a bit easier for me. In the parish hall we had quiz nights, talent contests and film shows.

Saturday nights were Tramps disco night. I'd only ever been to one disco, when I was fifteen, at the Charleville Lawn Tennis Club on the Whitworth Road. Some of the folk group in Cabra were members and I went down with my brother and a few others. I'd been told that there was a girl there who used to come to the folk Mass every Sunday, who liked me. At the end of the night I walked her home. We stood about one foot away from each other outside her house and talked for ages. I did like her but I hadn't a clue what to do. Was I supposed to kiss her or would she think that was really cheeky? And what sort of kiss? I'd never kissed anyone the way I'd seen some people kiss on the dance-floor that night. Would she be expecting something like that? I really didn't know. In the end I just said, 'Well, I suppose I better go home. See you in the morning at the folk Mass.' She looked like she wasn't expecting that.

At Tramps I helped out taking in money on the door or serving orange squash, lemonade and coke from the makeshift bar. Friends from school knew some of my new friends and we all stood around in a circle dancing. Audrey came with some of her friends and other fellas from school were there too. I was glad that people from school could see me doing normal things. I hoped that it would make me feel more comfortable around them but I was still very self-conscious and inhibited and couldn't let myself go. I liked dancing and wanted to enjoy it but I felt very nervous. Everyone else was so confident. Dancing, chatting, even laughing, all looked much easier for everyone else. I had noticed a girl, Deirdre, in the project during the week. She was smaller than me, fair-haired, and she wore nice bright clothes – pink skirt, white tee-shirt, short white socks and white runners. Deirdre chatted to me during the week and we danced at Tramps. Father Duffy had told the leaders that I wanted to be a priest and naturally others got to find out as well as the weeks went on. When Deirdre asked me about it I figured there was no point in even thinking about whether she fancied me or not. I liked her but I couldn't see myself with a girlfriend. And anyway I didn't think anyone would want to go out with me when they knew I wanted to be a priest. Not that there was anything wrong with wanting to be a priest, but it seemed to me that no one would really start a relationship that was obviously never going to lead to anything.

Some of my friends were in the folk group on the Navan Road and they sang at the half-eleven Mass every Sunday. I went to that Mass. And many times I went back for the half-seven Mass in the evening as well. I loved the Navan Road church. It was nice just being there. It felt clean, warm and real. Often I went into the church as I was passing, just to sit and talk to God or say a quick prayer. Before, I'd only ever said formal prayers and would never have gone into a church if there was nothing on. In Cabra I was so wrapped up in all the 'ancillary groups', as Father Payne used to call them, that it never occurred to me just to go round to the church to pray. Now I almost felt guilty if didn't go into the church. I thought of God as my friend and if I passed by his house without popping in to say hello I was being lazy and he'd be hurt. It was the same with the Rosary. Ever since I'd started going to Benediction on Monday nights I decided to say the

Rosary every night when I went to bed. Now I felt I had to do it or I was being bad in some way. When I was really tired it usually put me to sleep but I didn't think God minded that.

When the project was over I went abroad with the Catholic Youth Council. It was my first time out of Ireland and I was one of about 2,000 young people going to Rome to see the Pope. We would be the first group to have an audience with him since he'd been shot earlier in the year. We got the ferry to France and then had a long train journey to Rome. On the ferry I met Cardinal Ó Fiaich and shook hands with him. Bishop Casey visited every carriage on the train. He asked our names, told jokes, sang a song and then went into the next carriage. For the first couple of days we visited the sights and went to Masses in huge and beautiful churches. I bought presents for the family in Marks and Spencer.

We saw the Pope in his summer home, Castel Gandolfo, fifteen miles south of Rome. On a stage at the top of the garden there was Irish dancing and a folk group playing music. Bishop Casey was meant to be encouraging everyone to sing but he'd lost his voice because of all the singing he'd done on the train. The Pope walked down a path through the centre of the garden. We were all waving and cheering on either side of the path but for security reasons we had all been warned not to stand up. Two days later we were back in the Pope's garden because a couple from Limerick was getting married there. The Pope was not yet well enough to do a full wedding but after the ceremony a shiny black car pulled up in a corner of the garden and the Pope got out. I was almost getting used to seeing him up close. He blessed the wedding, thanked us for being the first people to visit him during his recuperation, and was gone.

I had had a great time but I was glad when it was over. Even on the train to Rome I had started to feel sad. I missed home and I missed my new friends on the Navan Road. I was worried about how much I would get to see them now that the project was over. I was looking forward to telling people about all that had happened on the trip. I couldn't wait to get home.

# 6. The Seminary

The next few months were lonely. I could not bring myself to study. Any time I tried I just couldn't concentrate. I looked forward to the weekends when I could meet my friends at Tramps on Saturday night and again on Sunday mornings when we all went into the parish centre for tea or coffee after Mass. But week nights were awful. Sometimes I walked up to the Navan Road and called in to Janet or Edel but I felt awkward. Although my new friends were great I thought they might think of me as a nuisance if I called in to their houses too often, so I walked around the area for ages hoping I'd bump into some of them. Then I went home pretending to everyone I'd had a great time.

I still had really bad feelings about myself and was very depressed. One night a few of us had got together for a small party in Janet's house. For weeks I had been wondering what would happen if I took eight or ten headache tablets. Would I die or would I just be very ill or what? I took about ten tablets to the party. I didn't think I wanted to die but I found living very difficult and needed to do something. I thought I might feel better if everyone knew how bad I was feeling and yet I didn't think I could tell anyone. I could have gone back to Ken Duggan but what I really wanted was for my new friends to know. And the fellas in my class in school as well. I thought that if all the people around me knew how badly I felt, without them knowing why, then somehow I might actually feel more comfortable with them. They might understand me or make allowances for me.

I went up to the bathroom in Janet's house. I had been thinking about it for so long that now I just wanted to do it. I had to do something about the way I felt. As I swallowed the tablets I had horrible thoughts about dying – dying that night.

'Don't think about it, don't think about it,' I told myself.

I went back downstairs and waited for something to happen. Already I felt much better. Soon I wouldn't have all these feelings, or if I did people would begin to realize I wasn't as happy as they thought I was and maybe that would help. It was like Russian roulette. Nothing happened at all and it was time for us to go. As I got nearer to home I was worried that if I went to sleep I might not wake up. Did I really want to die after all? I went back to Janet's house. There were still lights on and I knocked on the door.

'Andrew, you're back,' said Janet, looking surprised.

I tried to tell her what I'd done and just cried. She took me into the house and held me as we sat on the couch. Her parents decided that I should go to the hospital and another friend Paul took us there in his Mini. By the time the nurses sent me home I felt stupid and embarrassed. At the weekend I met my friends. I did feel a bit better because a few of them now knew that I wasn't well, that I was very unhappy. But I didn't tell them why.

In June 1982 I did my Leaving Cert. I managed to get some study done and luckily everything I'd studied for the English exam was on the paper. My mock Leaving had been terrible. That year, as the history paper was set out, you were given three major topics to discuss – like the Famine or the Industrial Revolution or Parnell – and then asked to choose from one of three associated subjects to link with them in your essay. It was sort of mix'n'match themes – so your essay would be called something like 'The Famine and the Catholic Church' or 'The Famine and Land Reform'. I picked the Catholic Church as my associated subject for each of my three essays. My teacher, Mr O'Hara, was not impressed.

'What's next – the Catholic Church and the Catholic Church?' he asked in front of the whole class. I hated him that day.

But that was all behind me now. The Leaving Cert class of 1982 left St Declan's in some style as we were all expelled about two weeks before the end of term for the most successful lock-out the school had ever seen. We blocked the doors to the four classrooms with tables, desks and chairs and closed all the windows. We were locked into the rooms for the afternoon and it took the staff ages to break in. And that was it. We were out and school days came to an end. Even though I'd found things difficult I still felt a little bit sad leaving Declan's but not for long. It was summer project time again and I was looking forward to it. I put off looking for a job until after the summer.

Earlier in the year I'd been to see the vocations director Father Corry Brennan. I was looking forward to meeting him and eager to see what he would say about me wanting to be a priest. The man behind the front desk at Clonliffe College brought me into a room just off the reception area and said Father Brennan would be with me shortly. It was great being back at the college – this time without Father Payne. Twenty minutes after the time of my appointment a tall, grey-haired man came into the room.

'Hello, Andrew, how are you?' he said, shaking my hand.

'I'm fine, thank you.'

He sat down opposite me. I was surprised that we were staying in the room. I thought he would have taken me into his office, presuming he had one. I was also surprised that he didn't have any information with him or a pen and paper to take notes.

'So, Andrew, you were telling me on the phone that you've wanted to be a priest for a long time. Would that be a couple of years, or longer?'

'Well, for as far back as I can remember really. Even as a little boy I just always wanted to be a priest. And then in recent years I've thought that the best way for me to live my life to the fullest would be as a priest. I love everything about priests' work and everything they do. I also very much believe in the Church and its teachings and agree with what the Church says on things like abortion, divorce and other things.' I went on to tell him about the work I had done in Christ The King church and my involvement now with the summer project. I told him the names of all the priests that I knew, hoping he would contact them and hear good things about me.

I didn't tell him anything about what Father Payne had done to me. I wondered if he knew already. When I telephoned and told him that I was interested in the priesthood, did he have to discuss my query with other people? And if so, could Father Stenson or Bishop O'Mahony, or anyone else that might have been told about my complaint, be one of these other people? I felt absolutely sure I was going to be a priest. And while I didn't think it was a good idea to mention what had happened with Father Payne to Father Brennan I really didn't believe that it would stop me from being a priest – I didn't think anything could after all the years I'd been preparing.

'Well now, Andrew, I think the best thing is for you to leave it for at least a year and then see how you feel. Go and get some work experience. You're only seventeen years of age, so there's plenty of time, and then we'll see how you feel next year. There was a time when we took people in straight after school but we don't do that any more.'

I had already been half-expecting this so I wasn't too disappointed. I knew that next year I could come back with my year's work experience and then I could start my training and learn all I needed to know to make me a good priest.

It was great to have the summer project on again – so many friends around for a full six weeks. I would be busy every day and wouldn't even have time to be on my own. Father Duffy had already left the parish and Father Eamonn Cotter from the All Priests Show, the 'singing priest', replaced him. Although I'd only known Father Duffy a short time I was very sad to see him leaving. I loved the way he said Mass and his sermons were great. He had such a passion when he was preaching. In him I had found someone who was a better example of priesthood than Father Payne had been. When I was younger I thought of Father Payne's casual clothes as a sign of him being with it and not old-fashioned. But now I saw it as an indication that he didn't take the priesthood seriously. I didn't think it was right that most of the time he was not clearly visible as a priest. I would let people know I was a priest twenty-four hours a day. That was the sort of life it was going to be. Father Cotter was in his early forties, had blond hair, wore navy instead of black, but had his collar on most of the time. I was surprised that some of my friends didn't like him. They thought he was too casual and maybe even insincere. In fairness, they had all been very close to Father Duffy who was a hard act to follow. I remember Father Cotter turning up late to one of our summer project meetings. It was obvious from what he was wearing that he'd just come from the golf-course and some of my friends didn't like it. Father Duffy would never have done that. I just thought it was good of him to come to the meeting on what I presumed was his day off. I liked him.

During the summer my father arranged an interview for

me for a job in a factory out in Coolock. After a short chat the personnel manager of Ross Portion Foods said the job was mine. The following Monday, just as the project ended, I started work as a quality controller in a frozen foods factory. I cycled out to Greencastle Parade in Coolock and went in to ask for Pauline O'Leary who was quality control manager. Miss O'Leary was a short, blonde-haired, middle-aged woman who was quite attractive and I presumed unmarried. She introduced me to Seán Deegan who was to be my immediate boss. He was in his mid-twenties, tall, dark, well-built and I imagined the girls would say handsome as well. I could see why. He took me all around the factory and showed me how everything worked. I was worried at having to remember so much but he told me I would have lots of help until I knew what I was doing. My job was to take burgers, grill-steaks and things like that off the factory line and check their quality. I had to weigh them, examine them for gristle and check that the colour of the packaging was within standards. Most of this could be done in our small office off the main factory floor where I worked with two other quality controllers, Pamela and Tom. Some of the work had to be done out on the factory floor, like emptying the metal detectors on each production line to check for food which had picked up tiny particles of metal when going through. As this passed through the metal detector it would be picked up and thrown into a basket, then I had to go through the burger and find the piece of metal. The factory floor was a busy place with people everywhere.

As the months passed, there were times when I felt okay and other times when I hated it. I hated when I became the centre of attention. I just couldn't handle it. Because the factory was divided into two parts, fresh and frozen, I was usually the only quality controller on my half of the factory at any one time. So if there was ever a quality-control problem it meant everyone looked at me. Sometimes the metal detector would be filling up really quickly and that drew attention to me as I stood there checking what was wrong. Sometimes I had to stop production because something was wrong and then everyone looked at me because they were on a bonus system and stopping production would affect their pay. Whenever they looked at me I just went bright red with embarrassment. I was easy to embarrass and they took full advantage. It became so bad that there were times when I walked out on to the floor that people looked at me to see if I would go red, and just because they were looking I would blush and then everyone laughed. As time went on it got worse instead of better.

Notions I had that I was different to everyone else seemed to be true. I just couldn't be like other people. It was me and them and they were normal. Most of the time I was nervous, always conscious of the fact that at any moment I could become the centre of attention and could be embarrassed and laughed at. I was all right when I was moving around or if I could avoid eye contact. But standing on my own at the metal detector, where I couldn't just walk away if I started to feel uncomfortable, I was trapped and could not avoid attention.

Although they slagged me, some of them liked me as well. Within weeks of starting work there, at the end of September, I turned eighteen. I got about forty birthday cards, mainly from girls, and a birthday cake which I had to balance on the handle-bars of my bike on the way home. Pauline O'Leary liked me as well because I was a hard worker and because she thought I was good-looking, at least according to Pamela. There were lots of girls working in the factory and some of them were really attractive. There was one girl who wore lots of make-up every day. Whenever I had to hand her back a packet of burgers she always made a point of stroking my hand. I was embarrassed but still it made me feel good – until someone told me that she did the same thing with all the new fellas. Another girl was having a twenty-first birthday party on a Friday night and invited me. I went along and someone bought me a pint of orange squash. They couldn't believe I didn't drink. Someone told me that the birthday girl fancied me and she sat beside me for all the time I was there. I didn't know what to do. I knew that if I stayed until the end she would soon realize how inexperienced I was so I made an excuse and left early.

Early in 1983 I started phoning Father Brennan again to get details of the entrance exam into Clonliffe.

'We haven't set a date yet. It's still only the beginning of March. If you want to get back to me in a few weeks' time I might have some news for you.'

'Could you tell me approximately when you think it might be?'

'Well, it would be before the summer but that's all I can tell you at the moment. Like I say, give me a ring in a few weeks' time and I should know more.'

I thought it was strange that he didn't ask about my Leaving Cert results, or how my job was going. In fact, he didn't ask me any questions at all. Maybe he'd already spoken to Father Finn or Father Duffy and they'd said positive things about me so he didn't need to ask me anything more.

I called Father Brennan another couple of times before getting an answer from him one Thursday evening when I phoned from work.

'Hi, this is Andrew Madden calling. I'm sorry to bother you again but I was just wondering if you had set a date for the exam yet.'

'Ah, yes, Andrew. Yes, em . . . the exam is on Saturday morning.'

'*This* Saturday morning?'

'Yes, that's right. Actually I was just going to phone you to let you know. If you can come down to Clonliffe College on Saturday morning – we'll start everyone at about ten o'clock so if you can be there about fifteen minutes earlier you should be okay. You know where the college is, don't you?'

'Yes, Father, I know where the college is.'

'Well, just come into the main reception. I'm meeting everyone there.'

'Okay, Father, that's great, thanks very much. See you on Saturday morning.'

'Bye.'

That was strange, I thought to myself. We didn't have a phone at home and I hadn't given him any number for work because I was never really near a phone. We had always agreed that I would phone him to find out the date for going to Clonliffe. So how was he just going to phone me? And how come he was just going to phone me when he had never tried to contact me before in all the time he knew I wanted to be a priest? And why had he left it so late? I had a horrible feeling that he hadn't planned to phone me at all. But I couldn't really believe that. As soon as he realized he didn't have my number he would have called up to the house and told me the date himself. Wouldn't he?

I cycled in through the gates of the college on the Clonliffe Road at half past nine on a damp Saturday morning and saw someone I knew walking through the grounds.

'Well now, Noel Kelly, I didn't expect to see you here this morning.'

'Well, here I am,' he said in his ever-so-posh accent. He hadn't changed in the year since we'd left school.

'Are you doing the exam at ten o'clock?'

'I am, yes, but it's not really an exam as such. It's just a lot of questions about you yourself so that they can try and ascertain what sort of person you are and whether or not you're suitable for the priesthood,' Noel told me grandly.

I locked up my bike and said I'd follow him to the reception area. In the big reception room where I'd met Father Brennan the previous year, three or four other young fellas, including Noel, were waiting. I sat down. Eventually a few others arrived and then Father Brennan came into the room.

'Good morning, everyone, I'm glad you could all make it. Is everyone okay? Yes? Good.'

After a short wait for latecomers we were taken up to a bigger room where there were chairs and tables laid out for us. Father Brennan introduced us to a younger man, who wasn't wearing a collar – probably a student there, I thought. He gave us out our first set of papers while Father Brennan left the room saying he would meet up with us again during the tea break. The test was to take about four hours with a break half-way through. I ploughed through the hundreds of questions, wondering if I should give really honest answers or just concentrate on making the best impression. One question was 'What do 16–18-year-old boys think about most?' I wanted to write 'Girls', given what I'd heard fellas going on about in school and up at the summer project. That would have been an honest answer and they might even recognize a budding sense of humour which would surely be a good thing. On the other hand, were they looking for something more serious like 'Jobs, careers and university'? The paper was full of questions like that and after I'd handed up one paper and was half-way through a second I came across the odd question that seemed just like one I'd answered an hour earlier. All I had to do was try to remember what answer I'd given.

During the break Father Brennan took us into another room for tea and biscuits. I stood talking to some of the other fellas and Father Brennan came over to say hello.

'Well, how did you all get on?'

'Okay,' said one person.

'Not too bad,' said another.

He asked whether any of us had come a long way. No, we hadn't.

'And what about yourself?' he said, looking at me. 'How are your exams going?'

'Exams?'

'Yes, isn't it the Leaving Cert you're doing this year?'

'No, Father, I did my Leaving Cert last year and passed it.'

'Oh right, so are you studying anywhere at the moment?'

'Well no, Father, I'm working in a frozen foods factory out in Coolock as a quality controller. I was talking to you last year and you said it would be a good idea for me to go and get some work experience.'

I was doing my best not to look as alarmed as I was starting to feel. Despite all my contact with him since last year and all the priests I gave as referees, it seemed that he hadn't a clue who I was. I wished he would start to take the whole thing a bit more seriously.

When the test was over he told us he would write with an appointment for each of us to go and see a psychologist at UCD. It was nothing to worry about, just a little chat. I went out to the university about two weeks later. The conversation was very short. The psychologist told me he had read through my paper and I could expect to see myself in Clonliffe in September. This was it. The priesthood at last. I could hardly wait. I never talked much about becoming a priest at home. Everyone knew anyway. My family had expected I would be going into Clonliffe that year but at least now it was kind of

official. Although it was still only May, my mother was planning a small party for the neighbours at the end of August. I
decided that I would leave work at the beginning of August
and have a month off to enjoy the project and see as much of
my friends as possible. I met Val at Mass on the Friday evening
and told her things were looking good. All I needed now was
to see Father Brennan and find out exactly when I would
enter the college and what the situation with money was. I
didn't think my father would have much to spare but I knew
that money would not be a problem if someone really wanted
to be a priest.

I had already told Pauline O'Leary at work about my plans.
She seemed very shocked. She asked me to let her know what
was happening as soon as possible because she would have to
find someone to take my place. I contacted Father Brennan
and he gave me an appointment to meet him at his house just
off Griffith Avenue one afternoon on my way to work. I was
looking forward to discussing the details with him. When
would I move in? What should I bring in with me? Should I
buy a collar and a black soutane? I knocked on his door several
times and waited for over an hour until I just had to leave or
I'd have been late for work.

I made a second appointment with Father Brennan. He said
he had no recollection of our first arrangement. Again I left
for work about an hour early and called in to him on the way.
This time he remembered.

'Hello, Andrew, come in, how are you?'

'I'm fine, thank you – and yourself?'

'I'm grand, thanks, grand,' he said, showing me into the
front room. 'Well, how are things with you?'

'Everything's going okay. As I said over the phone, I've
been to see the psychologist and I thought I should come to
see you now just to get the final word on my application.'

'Well now, Andrew, I've thought about it a lot but at the end of the day I think I'd have to say that I don't think it's for you.'

I must have misheard.

'Sorry?'

'I don't think it's a very good idea. I don't think it would be right for you at all.'

I could not believe what I was hearing.

'In what way would it not be right? I don't understand.' My voice trembled.

'Well, I can't really say. I just don't think it would be right,' he said. 'I'm sorry, but it just wouldn't be right,' he repeated as he stood up out of his chair.

'So is that it then?' I said desperately.

'I'm afraid it is. I think it's for the best.'

I couldn't believe this was the end. As I unlocked my bike from the railings in the front garden Father Brennan had already closed the front door behind me. I was in shock. I cycled to the factory and went straight up to see Pauline O'Leary. As the words came out I just started crying and couldn't stop. I cried for ages. She didn't know what to do. Somehow I didn't think she was used to teenage fellas crying on her shoulder. A few years earlier maybe, but not now.

She told me to go for a walk and not to come back until I felt better. I walked around Coolock on a miserable wet afternoon. What was I going to do? How could this have happened? I'd spent years working and helping out in the church and in the parish. I was an ideal candidate for the priesthood. Father Brennan had hardly spent any time trying to get to know me. How could he say it just wasn't right without explaining what he meant? Did he not realize how important this was for me, that this was my life? I felt shame. Everyone knew I wanted to be a priest. I'd never hidden it. I was proud of it. But now what was I supposed to say to people? In many ways I thought some people had always treated me a bit special because I was going to be a priest and I had enjoyed that. Now I wasn't following through, I felt like I was cheating. And what about Father Payne? He had left the parish in the middle of 1982 and had been given a new parish out in Sutton. The Catholic Church, which I had always loved, found him quite suitable to carry on being a priest – but I was not suitable at all. After all he had done. What the hell had *I* done? Why had I just been treated so badly?

I was upset and angry. I went back to work. Pamela and Tom tiptoed around me discreetly. Obviously Pauline had said something to them about leaving me alone today. They must have said something out on the factory floor because nobody bothered me much. On the way home I called in to my father's house and told him the bad news. He couldn't understand it. My mother was the same. On Saturday I went up to the parish hall on the Navan Road where my friends were preparing for one of the summer project shows that would be coming up soon. Val and I had become good friends. We went off together and I cried again as I told her what had happened. I went to see Father Maher and told him as well.

'Well, all I can tell you is he didn't come to me for a reference, Andrew, and I can't imagine why he didn't accept you.'

The decision seemed so final. And the future looked empty.

# 7. Drink

It was not going to be a great summer. Everything in my world had changed. I had never imagined myself as anything other than a priest. What was to become of me? From as far back as those Sunday mornings, carrying my surplice and soutane to the church to serve Mass, being a priest was all I'd ever wanted. And now it wasn't to be. I hadn't prepared for anything else. I went to Mass three times a week as usual but something was missing. I felt sad thinking that I would never be part of the Church in the way I had planned. Not only had I given the Church my youth but I had offered it my whole life and the offer had been turned down. It seemed that I just wasn't good enough. Or, I thought, good enough for Father Payne to use for three years but nothing else?

I was still looking forward to the summer project but only because my friends were there. It was no longer a case of being involved because of the link with the church. I could tell that Val had told the others what had happened. I was glad because it saved me from having to say anything. In June, before the project started, about ten of us went away for a long weekend. We rented a small house in Ballycreen, Co. Wicklow, a former school run as a holiday home by the Catholic Youth Council. Downstairs there was a large sitting-room, a kitchen, two bedrooms and separate toilets for girls and boys. Upstairs was just one big loft where we slept alongside each other in sleeping-bags. On the Saturday we went for a long walk and decided we would go to the local pub that evening after tea. I announced that I was going to drink for the first time.

'Andrew Madden, I'm surprised at you: you never drank before. I thought you were a Pioneer,' said Maeve.

'I was until now. But that was for a reason and now there's no point so I'm going to have a drink. Well, I'll try it anyway. You never know, I might not like the taste of it and never drink again but we'll see.'

'What are you going to drink – pints?' asked Val.

'I've never tasted alcohol so I don't know what anything tastes like. I don't think I want to drink pints. I don't know how anyone could drink so much liquid. I might try something else.'

As we sat in the pub that night Helen, Val and I decided to have brandy. Each of us had a neat brandy and knocked it back on the count of three. I could feel it hit the back of my throat then warm me up as I swallowed. I took a deep breath and breathed out slowly.

'Well, Andrew, how did that feel?' said Declan, a pint in his hand and a big smile on his face.

'Yes, that was nice. God, it's made me go all sort of hot.'

I looked at our empty glasses. Everyone else still had loads of their drinks left.

'Are we having another one?' I said.

'Let's wait until everyone else is finished and then we'll get another one at the same time,' said Val.

By the end of the night we'd had four neat brandies each, all knocked back. I'd had a great night, but by closing time I was drunk and in tears.

'I've had a lot of problems but youse have all looked after me. Youse are great friends, the best friends I've ever had. The only friends I've ever had. Youse have been great and I really like every one of youse,' I said as I cried my eyes out.

We set out for the long walk home with me draped over Helen the whole way. We got into our sleeping-bags in the loft, drunk and giddy.

'There was this fella called Tommy in his classroom in primary school,' said Val, 'and the teacher was asking everyone about their brothers and sisters and what their mothers and fathers did for a living. All the children had their hands up and one by one they spoke to the teacher. "My daddy's a policeman," said Paul. "Oh, that's nice," said the teacher. "My sister's going to be a nurse," said John. "Oh, that's great." Martin was next. "My mammy stays at home and looks after the house." "Oh, that's very important, mustn't forget the mammies – they work hard too. Okay, Tommy, what about your family?" said the teacher. "My sister's in university." "That's great, Tommy. And what's she doing at university?" "She's in a jar."'

Well, Val and I were in convulsions for ages. We thought it was the funniest thing we'd ever heard. Just as we thought we couldn't laugh any more, someone would say, 'She's in a jar,' and we'd be off again. Eventually we all fell asleep.

The following day we went to Clara Lara fun park where some of the gang enjoyed the assault course and other activities. I preferred just to watch. I was feeling more relaxed than since I was a child but I was still inhibited and self-conscious and didn't feel able to let myself go. We stopped off for a drink and bought some more to take back to the house. After dinner we sat around the table with several layers of jumpers on and played strip poker. I couldn't play poker and certainly had no plans to strip, but it was good fun and by the end of the night I was even drunker than the night before. I could barely walk, but two of the lads decided it would be a good idea if I went outside for some fresh air. As we walked down the small country road my legs went from under me and Ray carried me back to the house and up to the loft to sleep. The following day we all had a good laugh about how drunk we all were and I was glad I wasn't the only one.

Back at Ross Portion Foods things were as bad as ever. I had become unpopular with some of the workers and their supervisors because I was strict in applying the quality-control standards when some of them would have preferred me to turn a blind eye occasionally. This made me even more nervous and uncomfortable. And when I was being slagged I knew that some of the people laughing were really enjoying my embarrassment, and that made it even worse. I began to hate them trying to control me. Father Payne had controlled me and I wasn't about to let anyone hold such power over me again. If I gave in to the people in work and did things their way then they would have been in control, so unpopular as it was, I stuck to my guns.

I started to drink regularly in the evenings. I went up to Ned's on Blackhorse Avenue where I might catch one or two of my friends. I'd gone off brandy and started drinking vodka and orange. Drinking made me feel better. I could forget about all my difficulties. Forget about Father Payne. Forget about how different I was. Forget about how I just couldn't communicate or cope with other people. Forget about my self-confidence or the lack of it. I could escape from all of that and feel much better for a few hours. A lot of nights I ended up drunk.

There were arguments at home. I had started drinking in the house and my mother didn't like it, so I drank very little when anyone was in. Mainly I just went to Ned's and hoped someone I knew would be there. Mostly there was. A few of my friends from the project drank too and we got to know more people from spending so many nights down in the pub. Sharon McCormack was among them. She would be there at weekends. I liked her a lot. She was very attractive and she always gave me a smile when she saw me. I got the impression that she liked me as much as I liked her but it took me ages to pluck up the courage to ask her out. Eventually I did and she said yes. We had a couple of drinks in Ned's and then walked up to the Navan Road to get a bus into town. We were both tanned, blond and looking good that summer's evening. And I felt good inside.

As we walked towards the bus stop I met some fellas from school.

'How's it going, Andrew? Hi'ya, Sharon,' they said with big cheeky grins on their faces.

I felt great. Maybe I wasn't so different after all.

Sharon and I lasted about six weeks. We were out one night and she left early because she was tired. I wanted to go back to her house with her and watch television but she said no, she was tired and was going to bed. The following day it turned out that she had stayed up late watching a video with her brother and a friend of his. I took it personally. Instead of just accepting that she'd changed her mind, I thought that she went home because she didn't want to be with me and that she had got bored with me. I finished the relationship and then regretted it but I couldn't get her back after that.

In December I went to the Christmas party at work. I was drunk on arrival and got worse as the night went on. I kissed one girl for ages on the dance-floor and got my hand inside another girl's knickers after we went outside. Then I went back to the party and drank lots more. I argued with people I was usually afraid to talk to. I sat beside Pauline O'Leary's boss, Robert Carvill, and his wife, and talked absolute rubbish. After a while I realized I was being so loud that lots of people had stopped talking themselves and were all watching and listening to me. Even though I was drunk I was embarrassed. I fell out of the party having made a complete fool of myself. I met the company secretary, Mr Kelly, on the way.

'Is your face sore?' I said.

'No,' he said, looking confused.

'It's killing me,' I said, and stumbled out.

In February 1984 I left the factory after a row with one of the charge-hands. In one of my daily reports I had said that she was chewing gum on the factory floor even though I had asked her not to. Her supervisor told her what I'd said and she came to argue with me in front of other people, saying I hadn't told the truth. I felt myself panicking as people stood watching and I walked off. I told Pauline I'd had enough and walked out. Seán Deegan came to see me that night and I told him I should have been getting more support on the factory floor instead of being the only one out there making sure things were done to standard. I told him I would come back to work my two weeks' notice and then I was leaving. Robert Carvill asked to see me and told me that industry needed people like me, but my mind was made up. I couldn't wait to get out. That feeling of being trapped on the factory floor with so many people around would be gone for ever.

I signed on the dole at the Navan Road social welfare office. It was a horrible, filthy place. I always brought a newspaper to read in the queue because I was embarrassed people would see me and wonder why the priest-to-be was signing on. They gave me only part of my dole and said it would take a couple of months for the full amount to come through. As the weeks went on I had to borrow money from friends and I wrote cheques when I had no money in the bank. Soon I had a very big drinking debt, over five hundred pounds. I ignored it until I walked into Ned's one night and the manager, Mick, told me that the last couple of cheques he'd cashed for me had bounced. I nearly died. I told him I'd get the money to him as quickly as I could. I was embarrassed and I had no money so my friends bought me drinks.

Where the hell was I going to get over five hundred pounds? None of my friends would have that sort of money and if I asked anyone else they would want to know why I was drinking so much. Who could I ask? And then he came back into my mind – Father Payne. Of course. He always gave me the impression he had lots of money and, more important, if there was one person who wasn't going to ask me why I was drinking so much it was him. Val agreed to drive me out to Sutton. She knew something was wrong but when she saw I didn't want to talk about it she didn't ask any questions. We found the church, St Fintan's, and there was a large house right next to it. I knocked on the door and another priest answered. He told me Father Payne was out but would probably be back soon. I asked him to tell Father Payne that I was waiting for him at the front gates in a friend's car. Eventually I saw him walking towards us through the grounds of the church. I got out of the car and walked in his direction. As he got nearer I could see he looked very worried and I wondered if I was doing the right thing. Too late now.

'Hi, Andrew, is everything okay?'

I started crying. I hadn't seen him in nearly two years although it seemed longer. He looked older as well, greyer. I was also upset because when we were driving out I realized he was my only chance of paying my debts. If he couldn't help me then I was in big trouble, and not only that – I wouldn't be able to get served in Ned's while I owed them money.

'Has something happened? Is everything all right at home? Andrew, what's wrong?'

I didn't know where to start.

'Do you want to come into the house and tell me what's wrong?'

'Okay.'

'Will your friend be all right in the car?'

'Yes, she said she'd wait for me.'

Father Payne took me into his part of the shared house. I recognized the couch and armchairs. He must have brought them with him from the house in Glasnevin. I sat on the couch and he sat in an armchair to my left.

'Are you ready to tell me what's wrong?' he said quietly.

'Well, I've got myself into a bit of trouble. I owe some money to some people and now I have to pay it back and I can't afford it.'

'Are these people giving you trouble now?'

'No, nothing like that. It's just that I owe some money to friends, I'm overdrawn at the bank, I've written lots of cheques and I owe money in the pub.'

'The pub?' said Father Payne. 'I thought I could smell drink off you all right. So you've started drinking.'

'Well, that's basically why I've ended up in debt, I just can't help it,' I said, with tears streaming down my face again. 'I'm also expecting to get some money back from the dole office soon. I'm not sure how much that'll be but I'll be able to pay some of it back.'

'Well, don't worry about that for the moment.'

He wrote me a cheque for about five hundred and fifty pounds and handed it to me.

'Of all the people to have a drinking debt, I never imagined it would be you,' he said, with a big smile. I was so glad to be getting the money I didn't care whether he smiled or cried.

We chatted for a short while. Then I left, promising to get some money back to him as soon as I could. He was going out again 'to collect Pauric'. Who is Pauric? I thought to myself. Within a couple of weeks I received three hundred and thirty pounds back money from the dole office and took the bus out to Sutton. I left three hundred pounds in an envelope with Father Payne's name on it with the priest who opened the door. My other debts were paid so, apart from owing Father Payne £250, I was straight again.

I was involved in the project again that summer but my friends were not too happy when I turned up drunk a couple of evenings. Father Cotter told me I wasn't allowed to come up to the centre or the parish hall if I'd had a drink first. I could sense that those friends who rarely or never came to the pub were getting fed up with my drinking while the others didn't mind so much. I didn't drink for about seven days and then thought I'd start again, but trying to take it easier than before. After the project ended we were all up in the parish hall and I asked who was coming down to Ned's for the last hour before closing. Everyone said no. They were all going straight home. Janet said she'd come for a drink if I went for a short walk with her first. We walked into Ned's and saw a lot of familiar faces – the people who said they were going home for an early night were sitting in the pub. I was furious. I walked past them and went straight to the bar. Janet spoke to them and then came over to me.

'They said we should go over to them.'

'Well, you can go over if you want but I'm staying here. They all said they were going home and now look at them. Anyway, if you want to sit with them I'll understand,' I said, knocking back my first large vodka and orange.

'No, it's okay, I'll stay with you.'

I bought Janet a drink and ordered my second one. At the other end of the pub I spotted two people who used to be involved with the project. One of them, Derek, was planning to move to London. We went over to them instead.

In the short time before closing I got drunk. I glared at my friends on the way out, said goodnight to Janet and walked unsteadily down the Navan Road towards Cabra. As I got near the church I saw a young couple who came to the project in the evenings. They started laughing at me because I was drunk. 'I'll give them something to laugh at,' I thought to myself. I walked out into the busy traffic. Drivers were blowing their car horns and swerving to avoid me as I walked down the centre of the road. Next thing, Val's white Fiat 127 pulled up and some of my friends jumped out. Ray reached me first and dragged me over to the path. I was shouting at him to leave me alone. He raised his fist and punched me in the face, and I fell. It was the quickest way to shut me up. Val and a couple of others gathered round. They took me into Father Cotter's house where there was a small get-together for those who hadn't wanted to go to the pub. It must have looked like we'd brought the pub to them. I lay on my back on the floor. Father Cotter came in and out of the room. Ray was leaning over me, shouting.

'You drink too much and you know it, that's why we didn't want you to come to the pub. We just want to go for a quiet few drinks but you go to get drunk.'

'I don't get drunk all the time – just sometimes – and anyway I did try: I didn't have a drink for seven days,' I shouted back.

'Oh, well done, aren't you great, aren't you just great.'

I was livid.

'How the fuck would you like it if you were me, having things done to you, molested by a priest every week for three years? How the fuck would you like that, eh?'

The room was silent.

'You don't have to take my word for it, ask Bishop O'Mahony, he's coming here to say a Mass next week, isn't he? Well, ask him, he knows all about it.'

Nobody knew what to say or do.

'Val, will you give me a lift to see Father O'Farrell? I want to speak to him.'

Val agreed and Ray offered to come with us. The anger drained from me and I was no longer angry with my friends, just a bit upset. I could see Ray's point. I apologized to Father Cotter, saying it would never happen again.

Father O'Farrell was the priest in Cabra West who used to come in to school and talk to us. He had a strong Tipperary accent, was only in his late thirties, and wore his black suit and collar all the time. I used to think he was great. He would argue with fellas about religion and the Church and he took on anyone who had an opinion that was against the Church's teaching. One lunch-time he stood in the school yard as he and one of the fellas from sixth year argued with each other about 'the point of going to Mass'. They were surrounded by over 200 cheering pupils and it only came to an end when it was time for everyone to go back to class. Some days he would just walk around the school, knock on class doors and walk in. We always knew that meant the end of that subject for the day because he'd be in the class for ages. His phrase 'Keep the faith' became his nickname. I'd heard stories from his parish as well. On Saturday mornings if confessions were quiet, he'd go out to the church car park and drag in the fellas who were playing football outside to confess their sins. It was rumoured that once he stopped his car and got out when he saw a group of men gathered around two other men fighting. One of them said they'd hit him only he was wearing a roman collar. He went back to his car, took off the collar and went back to the same man who had a quick change of heart.

Now Father O'Farrell was in North William Street but in my drunken state I got it into my head that I had to see him, whatever time it was. There was no answer at his house. I was beginning to feel sick so I didn't want to sit in the car. I lay on the pavement outside his house with Val and Ray standing over me trying to persuade me not to fall asleep. The next thing I knew, Father O'Farrell was inviting us in. Ray and Val waited in the kitchen, having been told to make tea or coffee. Father O'Farrell took me into his front room and I told him what had happened that evening. He was shocked and I explained that the Church already knew everything. He told me to come down and see him during the week. I was sick in his kitchen sink, drank coffee to try and sober up, and slept in Val's car on the way home.

I went back to see him a couple of days later and repeated what I'd said already. He hoped the church knew what they were doing. Father Cotter asked whether or not I'd seen Father O'Farrell and if I was okay. He told me, 'Don't worry about being drunk in the house the other night, no hard feelings. Just look after yourself.'

# 8. London Calling

Over the next few months I thought about moving to London. I could not see myself as anything other than a priest in Dublin. I thought that I might feel better if I could leave all my problems behind. A fresh start. A new life. Three people from the summer project were there already so I wouldn't be alone. To save money I tried to cut down on my drinking. Culture Club was playing Wembley Arena in the middle of December and I was a big Boy George fan. I loved him for his outrageous clothes, his songs and his confidence. He was different and everybody loved him. I decided to go to London for the concert and stay on to see if I could find a job. A lot of my friends came down to Ned's on my last night. I knew I was going to miss them but I was excited about London – especially seeing Boy George for the first time. I didn't think about being away from home for Christmas. It wasn't going to be a very happy Christmas anyway – I had very little money and what I had I needed for London, not for presents.

On a wet Saturday morning I took the ferry from Dun Laoghaire, then a train down to Wembley Central station. Two friends, Derek and Barbara, were living nearby, off East Lane, and another guy from the Navan Road, Terry, was meeting me at the station. In the hour I was waiting for him I was amazed by the numbers of Asians, Pakistanis and blacks – I had never seen so many non-white faces before. Derek and Barbara shared their flat with an English girl and they said I could stay there for a while but unless a bed was free if one of them was away, I'd have to sleep on the floor or on the couch. Since I had only one hundred and twenty pounds with me I was glad of the offer. It would be a while before I could rent a place of my own.

The next morning I went job-hunting in the local pubs. Derek had said they would be looking for extra staff coming up to Christmas. I struck lucky in my second attempt – the place was almost empty and compared to Ned's it was tiny. This would suit me down to the ground. The man behind the bar was tall with dark greasy hair and a beer belly.

'I was wondering if you had any jobs going, even if it was just for the Christmas.'

He asked if I had worked in a pub before but when I said I hadn't he said it didn't matter, the work wasn't too hard. His name was John and he seemed friendly enough and he said I could start the following Wednesday.

That night I went back there with Derek, Terry, Barbara and her boyfriend, who I thought was a real hunk. Still on vodka and orange, I finished my first drink before everyone else. I decided to try drinking lager to make it last longer and go easy on my money.

'A glass of lager, please.'

'A pint or a half?'

'A glass.'

'Yes, but do you want a pint glass or a half-pint glass?'

'He wants half a lager,' said Derek from behind me, laughing. He then explained that a glass of lager meant nothing in English pubs, you had to ask for a half or a pint. I hoped John was right when he said it wouldn't be difficult working behind a bar.

The following night I went to Wembley Arena on my own and saw Boy George in concert. I didn't care that nobody else wanted to come: I knew I'd have a great time and I did.

On Wednesday morning I started work. It was mainly old men drinking pints of ale. It was busier at lunch-time with John's wife providing food. But on Friday night I realized how many people the small pub could hold. All the local lads were in and were determined to wind up the new barman. They called me Simon because Duran Duran was high in the charts and I had longish blond hair. I told them I preferred Boy George.

*Big mistake.*

'He's a bloody poofter,' they said. Who did they mean by 'he', I wondered. I found something to do at the other end of the bar.

By the end of January I'd had my first row with John. He said there was a discrepancy between the amount of alcohol sold over Christmas and the amount of money taken in.

He called me into his office. 'Before I go and speak to the other staff, can you assure me this is nothing to do with you?'

That I could just about take.

'You do realize you're employed in a position of trust.'

I saw red – I knew I had been very conscientious about handling the money – but I tried to stay calm.

'Of course I do.' I should have left it there, but I couldn't. 'And of course trust runs both ways, you tell me there's money or alcohol missing and I presume there is.'

'Okay, that's it, you're out, you can't talk to me like that.'

Over the next few weeks I insisted on meetings with everyone from the area manager right up to the managing director of the brewery but to no avail. But I had the satisfaction of knowing that John's employers must have realized that I wouldn't have gone to so much trouble if I hadn't thought I had been wronged.

After a couple of weeks working nights in McDonald's I

found a job with the Leisure Circle, based in Harrow. It was an international book and record club and I travelled around the Home Counties with a team of four others. We knocked on thousands of doors in hundreds of housing estates selling contracts for people to buy items from our catalogue. It was commission only, which was always a worry, not least because several nights after work we went drinking in the local wine bar. Most of the time I could handle the job. Though I met lots of people, generally it was one person at a time. Still, I sometimes stuttered dreadfully when they opened their doors and I had to deliver my sales spiel.

I was keen to lose my virginity but whenever the opportunity arose I made a quick getaway. When I had the pub job there was a dark-haired, curvy nurse called Deirdre who played Boy George on the pub juke-box and invited me around to dinner, but I wouldn't do anything more than kiss her. I liked Helen, one of the secretaries at the Leisure Circle. She was a short, cute, curvaceous blonde with a big personality. But I didn't think she'd be interested in me. She started going out with one of the other sales reps. At the Leisure Circle there was also Amanda. I kissed her, and slept with her when we were travelling overnight, but didn't have sex with her.

Now that I was keen to start some sort of sexual activity I became more insecure about my sexuality. I knew I was attracted to girls but I seemed to like fellas as well, though I never imagined sleeping with one. I didn't know any gay guys so there was never anyone around to consider approaching. And I ran away from sex with girls so quickly I certainly didn't think I'd have the nerve to sleep with a man.

So here I was in London, still feeling different from everyone else: I wasn't gay or straight, I was abnormal. There was a barrier between me and other people and I didn't feel able to break it down. So when there was a possibility of intimacy I couldn't handle it.

Six months after arriving in London I moved out of my friends' place in Wembley and into a flat with two nurses in neighbouring Pinner. In September I went home to share my twenty-first birthday with my twin sister, Audrey. It was great seeing all my friends again and at the party I wore a flamboyant outfit which was sure to get attention. The contrast between days when I felt happy and confident and those when I felt awful couldn't have been greater. A special occasion, like going home for the birthday party, would give me such a lift that I felt I could do anything. Dancing, making a speech, posing for lots of photographs in front of everyone, all came easily that night. I loved those days when I could stop being so serious about everything and just have a good time. Other times, I just wanted to hide in a corner and let someone else do all the talking.

After the New Year I left the Leisure Circle hoping to find something with a guaranteed regular income. Within days I got into the Civil Service as a casual clerical assistant. My first job was with Harrow District Land Registry. It was a large open-plan office with about twelve other people. At first I was quiet but gradually a few of them – Vicky, Jan and Caroline – became friends. When office banter turned a bit sarky my problems started again: the slightest put-down and I would think I wasn't liked. For days I would be on edge until something good happened. If they were nice to me, or if they asked me a question and I was able to help, they might say, 'Thanks Andrew, that's great,' and I'd decide they must like me after all. Until the next time.

If I became the centre of attention I blushed and they laughed. 'Oh look, bless him, he's gone all red,' and everyone would look up and laugh and give me a patronizing smile. I used to feel powerless and trapped. I couldn't just run out of the room. If I was feeling really well they couldn't make me blush at all and I was able to answer back. But how I felt seemed to be outside my control. To a lesser extent it was the same at my part-time job washing floors at Marks and Spencer in the early mornings. But there I didn't have much contact with people. I blew every hint of negativity or criticism out of all proportion and expected to be treated badly.

I moved into a bed-sit. I wanted to know I had to deal with people at night only if I went out or if I invited them in. Otherwise I could stay in alone and drink. Drink made me feel much better. I had to be in bed by half-ten because I was up so early every day and whatever I'd have had to drink soon put me to sleep.

There were so many attractive girls in the office that I couldn't help but think about sex a lot of the time. Some of the guys were cute as well but not many of them. There was a section in the local paper where people put in ads looking to meet others for love and romance – and the rest. At twenty-one I was desperate to lose my virginity and I came to believe that the best way would be with a total stranger. I knew girls fancied me but I felt that if they really knew me they wouldn't be so keen. And I felt so pathetic that I didn't want to have sex with someone who knew me. Eventually, after a few drinks, I phoned one of the numbers in the paper. Sara was twenty-five years of age, good-looking and blonde, and she drank half my scotch. Within a couple of hours of her calling to my flat we were finished. I had enjoyed her body and I felt more normal than I ever had. I also wondered if I'd been any good. We made no arrangements to meet again.

Although it was a drunken affair I felt great afterwards. I

couldn't stop thinking about it for days. For a short while I thought I was becoming more normal by the day. But it wasn't long before my confidence was slipping again. However, my work was fine and I had been made permanent, so my problems were not attracting undue attention from my bosses.

I started going out with an Irish girl from the office, Susan. She was of medium height, had long brown hair and a great figure. The only annoying thing about her was her cackle of a laugh. She was so attractive that I'd never have asked her out if she hadn't made it so obvious she fancied me. From the first time I smiled and stared at her she always made a point of coming over for a chat, and one day she came back from lunch with chocolate for me – 'because you're so nice'. I couldn't believe my ears. She agreed to go out with me. We would go back to my place and roll around on the bed kissing passion-ately, fully clothed. We started to undress many times but I always put a stop to it. I couldn't work out what was wrong. We agreed to split up one morning standing beside the coffee machine at work. It had lasted about six weeks.

I became very depressed but couldn't understand why. These bouts of depression and my lack of confidence meant I dreaded going to work some days. I wanted to be on my own, not surrounded by lots of people in a busy office.

I was working long hours and enjoyed drinking in the evening. Often there were parties and other social occasions to go to with friends from work and I enjoyed most of them because I could relax with a drink. Having had sex, I was keen to have another go. And now I was ready to try it with a man. It was difficult to imagine it happening – but not long ago it had been difficult to imagine being with a woman, so I wasn't about to be put off. There were lots of men I found attractive, so I didn't have any particular type in mind. I bought a copy of the *Gay Times*. Even though I was comfortable with what I was doing I still stood outside the newsagent for ages waiting until I would be the only customer. I was amazed at the classified ads: one guy after another describing themselves and all looking to contact other guys. Maybe it wasn't so unimaginable after all.

I replied to an ad and after a few weeks I had a letter and a telephone number. I thought about it for over a week and then phoned. He said his name was John and he was Italian. We chatted for a while and agreed to meet. I couldn't think of a venue where I wouldn't meet someone I knew, so I asked him to come to the flat and have a few drinks.

I was in heaven. Large muscular build, dark hair and drop-dead gorgeous. My broad smile must have given me away. We chatted over drinks, then he made his move. He was passionate and strong and God, I wished I had a body like his. Soon afterwards he left. He didn't ask for my number and said I could call him if I liked, but he wasn't looking for a relationship. It had never occurred to me that I might have a relationship with a man and I never called him again though I did think of him a lot.

Tony Ward caught my eye at work. I didn't fancy him but he was handsome in Doc Marten boots, black combat trousers, long white shirts and always a black leather jacket with Cabaret Voltaire across the back. By now I often wore very loud clothes and people couldn't believe the change in me since I'd first arrived. I loved the clothes from the Boy shops in Carnaby Street and on the King's Road. I was a walking contradiction: some days not wanting any attention, and then arriving into the office looking like a pop-star. One night I went to the Railway Bar in Harrow wearing an exact replica of the outfit Boy George wore for his infamous appearance at the huge anti-apartheid concert on Clapham Common in June 1986, when he was so spaced out the world knew he was on drugs for sure. The Railway Bar was always busy with punks and office types – everyone usually looking at the punks. That night the punks were looking at me. Again I had created an image, a brash front for the real me to hide behind. I knew some people thought I looked hideous, but if I changed then they would have been in control.

Tony and I got talking and agreed to go for a drink in Hobbs wine bar at lunch-time. I had lager, I didn't want to overdo it. I had become fond of scotch and coke but I'd had plenty of that at home over Christmas and in January 1987 I promised myself I would try to drink a little less. As soon as the effects of an excessive Christmas wore off, I changed my mind. Tony and I became good friends and we had two or three pints together nearly every lunch-time. Often I needed a couple of whiskies as well. I still spoke to Vicky and Jan but we were working in different parts of the building now and that helped me maintain a distance. I didn't trust them not to be loud, particularly Vicky, and they enjoyed embarrassing me so much that I wasn't really that keen to see them except out socially as part of a group.

Because I was up and down so much I spoke to the Welfare Officer at work, Gay Furnell. I never told her anything about the past so I knew she wouldn't really be able to help, but at least she was there to talk to. I was now drinking at least five bottles of scotch a week and with rare exceptions could hold it well. I spoke to a doctor at Northwick Park Hospital about my drinking and she gave me a month's supply of Antabuse as I thought she might. She told me to take one tablet a day and that if I drank at all I would be extremely ill. Unfortunately Antabuse didn't take away the desire to drink, nor did it deal with all the horrible feelings I had about myself, so I had little motivation to take it. I kept the tablets for a time when my depression became really bad again. I tried to persuade one of the girls in work, a diabetic, to give me a syringe. I wouldn't tell her what I wanted it for and she was suspicious and wouldn't oblige. I'd heard that if you injected an empty needle into yourself, the air could cause you to die or at least have a heart attack. I wanted that needle for the next time I felt low.

Eventually, when I was going through another bad time, I went to the canteen in the afternoon when it was quiet, made a coffee, poured the month's supply of tablets into the cup and drank it. I didn't care what happened to me. Part of me was still, after all these years, trying to let people know how much I was hurting. And part of me was being more destructive than that. I had no way of knowing what the effect of so many tablets would be. I had been to the wine bar that day so I expected a reaction.

Nothing happened, though I have no recollection of that night. The following day I went for a drink at lunch-time. As I drank my first pint people started to stare. The staff asked if I was all right and then stood huddled together nearby. I could see my reflection in the mirror. My face was going purple and all the white in my eyes was dark red. I went back to the office and sat at my desk. A colleague rushed over.

'Are you all right, Andrew?'

'Yeah, I'm fine.' I still felt all right.

'Oh no you're not,' she said. People were beginning to notice. 'Come into the welfare office and I'll find Gay Furnell.'

I sat on the bed in the office and Gay Furnell looked into my eyes.

'I don't like the look of you one bit,' she said.

'Thanks very much,' I said.

I was beginning to feel tired and lay down. When I woke, the personnel officer, Gay and two ambulance men were standing over me. In the hospital they made me vomit everything up. The place stank like a brewery. I slept for hours. When I woke during that night a nurse brought me a reheated dinner and sat chatting for ages, me in tears. Within a couple of days I was back at work, feeling fine, and told anyone who asked that antibiotics for an upset stomach had clashed with a drink, hence the ambulance, and yes, wasn't it awfully silly of me.

Everyone noticed Mayanie Wicker. She knew Tony and Vicky but the two girls did not get on. Mayanie was from Sri Lanka. She was dark-skinned, long-haired and always wore nice make-up. She wore short skirts, stockings and high heels and I fancied her like mad. John may have been good but Mayanie was stunning. Any chance I got, I chatted her up. Vicky could see what was happening and said she'd never speak to me again if I went out with Mayanie. I couldn't believe my luck – talk about killing two birds with the one stone. Mayanie and I got on really well. At first we kept it quiet. We knew Vicky was leaving soon and I didn't want her giving Mayanie any trouble at work with her big mouth. In the end it wasn't long before everyone knew. Despite ourselves, we were too obvious. Tony started going out with another girl from work, Natalia, so we made up a good foursome for going out on Saturday nights. During the summer we all went to Cyprus. The boys on the beach thought Mayanie was cute in her sexy bikini. I thought *they* were cute. Pale and not-very-interesting Natalia looked like she'd spent the two weeks in hospital. And otherwise cool Tony, who couldn't swim, was just relieved we made him get in the pool only once.

After about six months I started losing interest in sex with Mayanie. At the same time I loved her more than I'd ever loved anyone. I had never shared so much of every aspect of my life before. We had lots in common: loud music, clubs, drinking (me more than Mayanie), taking chances (passionate kisses in the office lift), staying in bed for hours on Sunday mornings. But I didn't really want to continue the physical side of the relationship. In fact, it annoyed me to see someone I had such strong feelings for being interested in sex. I felt she should have known better. Whenever we had sex, especially if I initiated it, I knew I was using her for a physical release and I didn't like it because I loved her so much. I tried to end the relationship but she wouldn't have it. She could turn on the tears and she knew it would get to me.

Everything came to a head in 1989. It was a horrible year. While I hated being in work I was actually doing my job very well – probably because I kept my head down. I was asked to apply for promotion but didn't expect to get it on my first attempt, so I put the interview down to experience. I was off sick for the day when Mayanie phoned to say I'd made it to executive officer. I'd joined only three and a half years earlier as a casual clerical assistant and some people had been there ages and had failed many times. I was delighted, but not for long. Promotion meant I couldn't choose to keep a low profile. I would be running any one of half a dozen large open-plan offices where I might be the centre of attention – whether I was able for it or not. How could an executive officer who was so easy to embarrass and intimidate have control? I went back to work for a few weeks but left the job after another period of sick leave.

I moved to another flat. I owed money all over the place and didn't want to be found. I started working for Abbatts

Employment Agency in Victoria Street, just opposite the train station. I was sent to work as a porter in a block of luxury flats in Sloane Square. It was only temporary and the money wasn't going to be enough to live on. I had lost my licence for driving over the limit and had sold my car. Instead of paying off the car loan, I cleared other debts, wasted some money and left a small amount in the bank. I knew the finance company would find me sooner or later and I had no way of paying it what I owed.

All I drank now was scotch – about seven bottles a week – mixed with coke. Mayanie's mother was amazed to see me drink a full bottle of scotch during the course of a day and then go back to the off-licence for more in the evening. And yet in the time she knew me she saw me drunk only once.

Sometimes Mayanie shouted, she was so angry that I wanted to end the relationship. Other times she just cried and I hated myself for hurting her. How could I do this to someone I loved so much? But, at the same time, how could I stay in a relationship that just wasn't working? My lack of interest in physical intimacy had put a huge strain on both of us. We were having rows about everything but sex, though that was the real issue. After two and a half years we finished – in August 1989. There had been arguments, silences and tears. But there was love, trust and laughter as well and we were both faithful to each other the whole time.

I wanted to get away from everything. I knew that if I stayed in London the relationship with Mayanie would be in the background. It hurt me to see how much I had upset her and I would never really be able to walk away. I was just getting into more debt as well. I felt like I was suffocating with everything going wrong around me. And so much of it was my own fault. I had about three hundred pounds cash and decided to go home to Dublin. Mayanie offered to pay for my flight if I stayed another day, and I agreed. It was a small amount compared to what I already owed her.

# 9. Visiting the Bishop

It felt good to be back in Dublin. I signed on the dole at the Navan Road Labour Exchange again. It was still a dump. I was glad that the signing-on time they gave me was really quiet, and I was out of the place in a couple of minutes. I joined the City Gym off Abbey Street and went at least three mornings a week: I wanted to get healthy and put on some weight. I tried to look bigger by wearing baggy tracksuit bottoms and over-sized tops and jumpers. I made myself eat lunch every day and spent the afternoons scouring the papers for jobs. I sent out my curriculum vitae to absolutely no avail. Secretly I was glad it was so difficult to find work: I might not be able to cope with people. In the late afternoon I went to the Hole in the Wall pub on Blackhorse Avenue and acquired a taste for Guinness. I drank three or four pints over a couple of hours and went back at night and drank with whoever was around.

Except for never having enough money to last the week, it was a good six months. I had great nights out with friends. I met several girls and enjoyed one-night stands. I rarely slept with the same girl twice because I knew that if I got to know her I would lose interest. I looked at guys but didn't dare act on any impulses. Although I'd already slept with one man I wasn't sure it was something that was going to happen again, especially in Dublin. There were one or two gorgeous-looking guys in the gym but I assumed they were straight. I missed Mayanie. At least, I missed the times when everything was good between us.

Since I wasn't working I didn't find myself trapped in so many awful situations. The only time I was nervous was when I walked into the pub in the afternoon. If it was quiet I was grand and relaxed. But if it was busy I became very tense, so tense I could barely pick up my pint. It wasn't that my hands would shake, but I'd hold the glass so tightly I was afraid I might crush it. After one or two pints I'd calm down. I'm sure the alcohol helped to calm me but it was also psychological. After I'd picked the pint up several times I'd keep telling myself, 'Relax, you haven't smashed or dropped the glass and your hands haven't shook and none of these things have ever happened – so relax,' and eventually I would. Still, the following day I was nervous if the pub was busy, and I had to go through the whole thing again.

Being in Dublin, being so on edge and missing the emotional support of the relationship with Mayanie made me think about Father Payne a lot. I felt sure that if I'd never met him I wouldn't be finding life so difficult. I assumed I was the only person he had molested but I could never be sure. He took a big chance with me after all: he had a good job and a nice house and car, yet he put it all at risk. The Church had kept him on but it might not have, and then he would have lost everything. If he liked abusing boys, would it have been so easy for him just to stop when I told on him? And why was I not suitable for the priesthood? Of course I no longer wanted to be a priest – I had found a new life, difficult though it was, and my vocation had died – but the question was still there.

I found Bishop O'Mahony's number in the directory. A woman answered the phone. I hoped she wasn't going to be one of these over-protective housekeepers who wasn't going to let just any member of the common laity speak to a bishop. But she was friendly and Dr O'Mahony took my call.

'Hello, Bishop O'Mahony, my name is Andrew Madden,

I'm calling from Cabra. I used to know Father Payne a few years ago. I don't know if my name means anything to you.'

There was a brief silence.

'Yes, Andrew, indeed I think I do remember the name, how are you?'

'I'm very well, thank you. I was wondering if I could possibly make an appointment to come to see you?'

'Indeed you can, just let me have a look in my diary. When did you have in mind?'

'Well, you're busier than me, so whenever is a good time for you.'

'I know it's a few weeks off but would it be awful if I left it until mid- or late October? Would that be too far off for you?'

'No, not at all.'

A few weeks later I was sitting in Bishop O'Mahony's lounge in his home in Swords. I was amazed at the number of books on tables and desks in the room. The Bishop wore a black suit with his collar. The only indication of his rank was a few framed photographs taken at a wedding. I said no thanks to tea or coffee. I couldn't have held a cup still because as usual I had been drinking the night before. We sat in comfortable armchairs facing each other and I told him about how recent years had been for me. He listened carefully. I asked about the decision to turn me down from the priesthood. He was sure it was nothing to do with my allegations against Father Payne, but he didn't actually know why. He promised to look into it and get back to me but doubted that records had been kept.

I asked him how he could be sure that Father Payne wasn't abusing anyone else. He insisted he had no reason to believe that he was. I put it to him that when I was being abused he had no reason to believe it was happening then either. But it was. Bishop O'Mahony repeated his earlier answer. Despite his words and his warm smile, I remained unconvinced.

He saw me to the door after exactly one hour. I was glad to have met him. I felt better that someone in his position had heard how Father Payne's actions were playing havoc with my life as an adult. But I could tell that our conversation would have no effect on Father Payne.

After a few months of eating well and going to the gym I'd gone from nine to ten and a half stone. The absence of stress and the easing of depression did a lot for my self-confidence. I started to feel a bit better about myself and decided that if there were no jobs to be had in Dublin I should go back to London. I was capable and deserved better than Dublin's dole queues.

I phoned a friend in London and asked her to send me a copy of the *Evening Standard* so I could look for flats and jobs. I had enjoyed the short time I'd spent in Sloane Square so this time I wanted to move right into the centre of London. I looked for flats in the SW1 area. Over the phone I booked one in Pimlico. I was disappointed to be leaving my friends again but I knew it was for the best. I wrote to the Civil Service and told them I wanted to be reinstated but I wanted a position in the centre of London. Abbatts told me that they would be delighted to take me on as a temporary porter again so I knew I'd have work there as well.

I arrived in Pimlico in February 1990 and paid my new landlord a deposit and six weeks' rent in advance. I had very little money but at least I had a roof over my head. And a roof was about all it was. I scrubbed the tiny room as much as I could but it never really felt clean and the bathrooms were awful.

Abbatts found me two evening jobs. One was at Bolebec House in Belgravia, just twenty minutes' walk from my flat. It was a block of twenty-five luxury flats and I worked alone there Friday to Sunday, from four in the afternoon until midnight. My job was to be porter, security man and receptionist all in one. After a few weeks the management at Bolebec House offered me a permanent position doing the same hours. The second job was a similar position just two minutes from Bolebec House, working six hours from five in the evening, Monday to Thursday. The Lord Chancellor's Department (LCD) said it would give me a job. But it would take several months before a position was available so I had to do something else during the day. I found two cleaning jobs, doing offices and toilets in a place on the King's Road from six to half-nine every morning and, after breakfast, cleaning rooms and toilets in a small guest-house off Sloane Square until lunch-time.

I was delighted: I had eighty hours of work a week, all within walking distance of my flat. I had a couple of drinks at lunch-time and nothing more until I came back to the flat at midnight. I was exhausted by the end of the day and didn't really have time to drink my usual amount. I was also glad to be spending so little time in the dirty house. There were some Japanese girls living there and I got to sleep with one of them on a regular basis. She didn't want a relationship, just sex, and I wasn't complaining. After she moved away I started sleeping with her friend, who was of a similar frame of mind and body.

Generally I felt comfortable in my new jobs because I spent so much time alone. As a porter my dealings with people were mostly on a one-to-one basis and I could cope. Sometimes my nervousness came back to haunt me, but things were going so well for me that most of the time I felt good and could beat it. In August, the LCD was ready for me and I took up the position of administrative officer in the superannuation section. I had to give up the promotion to executive officer I'd received at the Land Registry because I hadn't taken up the position. I gave up the cleaning jobs and kept on the evening jobs, so I was still working eighty hours a week.

My immediate boss in the LCD was Helen, a tall, slim, blonde girl from Yorkshire. Apart from me, there were nine people in the section and I hoped I would be all right. There were at least twenty others working in the same open-plan office but I had my back to them so I didn't feel too nervous at first. I thought I could pretend they weren't there. I took to the work well and was acknowledged as being good at my job – a boost to my confidence. A grey-haired Scottish woman in her fifties ran the section and she had a talent for drinking coffee, eating an apple, smoking a cigarette and farting all at the same time. The only thing she didn't do was blush.

By Christmas I was working five nights a week, Wednesday to Sunday, at Bolebec House. The other porter's job had ended. I enjoyed being busy and earning good money. With such a prestigious location – Harrods was just five minutes' walk away – Bolebec House was a much sought-after apartment block. It was one of the few blocks where the porters were on duty twenty-four hours a day. So many porters in the area were elderly men that we all stood out, being young and smartly dressed in our navy suits. The residents were amazed that we were all doing other things outside of work: Buffy was studying economics; Marcus was into God and accountancy; the head porter, Magnus, always had some entrepreneurial scheme up his sleeve, and I was at the LCD.

I was still limited in the time I could spend drinking every day so I relished it all the more when the opportunity presented itself. In the New Year I paid Mayanie back all I owed her with interest. I was visited by a bailiff who told me I was being sued by the company which had financed my car loan. They had tracked me down as I knew they would. I contacted them and made arrangements to clear the loan. In April I moved out of the filthy house and into a nice refurbished one on St George's Drive, also in Pimlico. The accommodation was still only one room but it was large and all the furniture was new. I lay in bed on the first night contemplating how lucky I was. My debts were manageable, I'd come from seventy pounds a week dole money to an annual salary in excess of twenty thousand pounds and rising, and now I had a nice place to live. I didn't want to sleep. I just wanted to stay conscious of how good things felt.

But it wasn't all good. Working back in an office was presenting the usual problems. Sometimes I coped really well, other times I could barely face work because I felt so insecure. I developed techniques to help me cope with difficult days. If everyone was talking together in the office, and I felt myself panicking because I thought the conversation was going to turn to me, I would pick up the phone on my desk and make a call; I knew my colleagues would not speak to me while I was busy. The time spent on the phone was usually enough for me to calm down and I would be all right afterwards. Sometimes I went out to the toilet, or upstairs to use the photocopier, just to give myself a couple of minutes to catch my breath and calm down. Of all my anxieties there was only one which was real in as much as what I was anxious about happened on a regular basis: sometimes someone would make a comment about the Irish and people would look to see if I was going to respond, and I hated becoming the centre of attention in that way. I would panic and become embarrassed and when people laughed I felt my vulnerability was being exploited.

Other fears were not so well founded. I didn't have to use the Underground much but I hated it when I did. I always took a newspaper with me so I could avoid eye contact with people. All too often if you looked around the Tube you would catch someone's eye, and then you would look back at them to see if they were still looking at you only to find that they were doing the same thing, and I found that embarrassing. And if you sit on the Tube going red for no apparent reason people are going to notice and then you'd have even more people staring at you, so if I wasn't feeling good I always took a newspaper. Very rarely did I get chronically embarrassed on the Tube: just like my worry about crushing the glass in my hand when I was feeling tense in the pub, I was anxious about something that rarely or never happened. It was the same when I had to cash a cheque in the bank or use a banker's card in a store. I could feel myself getting nervous as I stood in the queue and if the cashiers asked me to sign the back of the cheque I was afraid they would see how sweaty my palms were and that my signature would go all wrong because I was so tense. Of course the cashier never questioned my signature. The fears were imaginary but the anxiety they caused was very real. And so alcohol played its part – releasing the stress and worry and making me feel much better about myself.

On Monday nights I started going to the Limelight, a club on Shaftesbury Avenue. I had been there many times with Mayanie on a Saturday night but in much of Soho and the West End Monday night was gay night. I didn't fancy going to new places on my own. The Limelight, which used to be a church, was always packed, and I wanted to relive the great night I'd had with the Italian stallion, John. In the basement they played stuff from the Seventies and Eighties. On the ground floor it was more up-to-date, with house and garage music. Upstairs was a dark balcony area where people could get to know each other better – snog – or just watch all the action on the dance-floor.

The guys were young and handsome so I was spoilt for choice. Not that I did much choosing. I didn't have the nerve to approach anybody. The best I could do was try to make eye contact with someone I fancied and hope that if they felt the same way, they would come over to me. Sometimes I was left standing, other times I got lucky. I preferred to bring people back to my flat because I felt more in control of the situation. I slept with some guys more than once but usually I preferred not to. I had a feeling that once it was over that was it: we had used each other. If I met someone again at the Limelight I was always happy to talk and be friends, but nothing more. Most guys were happy enough with that, although occasionally someone would be offended and pass you with their nose in the air like a wounded peacock.

I knew I was living a lonely life. Sometimes I only went to the Limelight for company but that usually came in a package which inevitably included sex. I hadn't forgotten the sexual problems I'd had with Mayanie. Nor had I forgotten how much I'd hurt her by ending the relationship. After I'd been sleeping with one of the Japanese girls for three or four months the problem had recurred. In her case we weren't really friends: I just went to her flat after work on a Saturday night, we played music, chatted, had a few drinks and then spent the night together. But it wasn't long before I saw her as more than just someone to have sex with, and once I developed those feelings I didn't want the sex because I knew I was just using her. So at the Limelight I was avoiding relationships and building up lots of casual friendships, guys to chat to when I arrived. I was scathing of anyone who actually wanted to go out with me. So little did I think of myself that I wondered why anyone would really want me as a boyfriend. Why were they settling for so little? Did they not realize how much better they could do? If they wanted me there must be something wrong with them too.

Although I should have, I still didn't consider myself exclusively gay: there had been a lot of girls, and I had enjoyed them, but by now I knew I preferred guys. I didn't tell anyone but it wasn't out of shame that I said nothing. Rather, my sexuality, whatever it was, didn't bother me that much. I wasn't afraid to tell people at work either – my boss, Helen, and another colleague, John, had become good friends – but I just didn't want to stand out for any reason and chance drawing attention to myself on those horrible days when I couldn't handle it. So it was fear of anxiety rather than fear of homophobia that kept me in the closet.

I felt very sure that had I never met Father Payne I would be living a much happier life. Feeling so different, keeping people at a distance and being lonely and so frequently depressed, nervous and anxious – all of this I attributed to my experiences with him. He always came to mind whenever I considered how difficult I found life. Even the happy times were marred by the knowledge that contentment would never last, that those dark days were bound to return. He had inflicted so much damage on me and nothing had happened to him. In fact, he had been removed from a working-class parish and sent to one of the wealthiest parts of Dublin. I could imagine him showing off the fact that he lived in Sutton. It would add to his sophisticated image. But then, although he'd never apologized maybe he really was sorry. I didn't think so but I had no way of knowing.

And what about the Church? It had allowed him to carry on as a priest. Years ago that hadn't surprised me but now it seemed very wrong. I had received no acknowledgement or apology for what had happened to me and instead of feeling better and stronger as the years passed I seemed to be getting worse. Materially I was doing well. But what about how I felt inside? I was often so unhappy. Sometimes I just came home from work after midnight, poured myself a large drink, sat beside the blaring stereo and cried. I was empty and everyone else seemed so happy. I knew people had problems, I wasn't stupid. When I was signing on a year earlier, just after I returned to London, I'd seen wretched Irish people in the dole queue at nine in the morning, drinking cans of cheap lager. I passed that dole office on the way to work and the same faces were there every week. I didn't have their problems. And I saw couples coming home late at night shouting and arguing with each other and I appreciated how nice it was for me to go back to my flat knowing I didn't have to face a marriage that was long dead. But somehow their problems seemed soluble. Mine didn't. I had no hope.

I'd seen television programmes about the Catholic Church in America being sued by young people who had been abused by priests when they were younger. The Church had paid them compensation running into millions of dollars. It seemed to matter what had happened to those people. I also became aware of what is now known as the 'pindown' scandal. A report published in May 1991 said that children in care in homes run by Staffordshire County Council had been deprived of the right to leave the homes. Every day they had to wear their night-clothes or pyjamas to make sure they didn't leave the building. There was no physical or sexual abuse but it was still deemed unacceptable that the children had been treated in this way. There was talk of the social workers being sacked and the children being compensated. It wasn't that the money was going to undo any of the harm, but paying compensation was society's way of making amends to someone who had been hurt or damaged in some way by a public institution. Like the American cases, what had happened to these children was taken seriously, and those responsible were brought to account and obliged to pay for their past negligence.

Was I any less important than these other people? Did it

not matter that I too had been hurt? Bishop O'Mahony hadn't got in touch as he'd promised. Since it had known about Father Payne's abuse the Church had shown no regard for what had happened to me and my suffering was continuing. Maybe I could take the opportunity to say actually it does matter, you can't screw up my life and just walk away.

# 10. Taking Action

I thought about it for weeks. Had I left it too late? Should I use an Irish solicitor or one in London? Was this really such a good idea at all? Plus I had no real proof. Though there was my old teacher, Ken Duggan – he knew. But would he still be interested after all these years? I felt sure he would. And what about Bishop O'Mahony? I couldn't imagine he'd lie on the witness stand.

Stephen, a friend from the Navan Road, had some business in London and he stayed with me for a week. We stayed up late chatting over a bottle of scotch. We always had a good laugh when we got together, arguing politics and talking about girls. (I didn't dare tell him I was gay: I still wasn't sure of it myself – although by now sex with girls was a thing of the past.) I knew that if I told Stephen my plans he would give me an honest opinion; playing to the gallery was not his thing. He wasn't at all surprised to hear about the abuse. 'I knew it, I just knew it,' he kept saying.

When he went back to Dublin he sent me the names and numbers of some solicitors. I phoned a few of them but nobody seemed interested in taking the case. Eventually one solicitor suggested trying Alan Shatter TD, saying, 'He would be interested in that sort of thing.'

On 20 June I contacted Gallagher Shatter Solicitors but Mr Shatter's secretary told me that he was very busy and not taking on any new cases. She offered to put me through to Tim O'Sullivan, another solicitor in the company. I outlined my story nervously. He said I might have left it too late but offered to get a further opinion from a senior counsel, Gerard Durcan. I was pleased with that. At least he hadn't turned it down straight away, so there was some hope.

In September Tim wrote looking for more details of my allegations for Gerard Durcan. I was happy that things seemed to be moving, albeit slowly. Obviously they thought the case was worth investigating. By the end of October Gerard Durcan confirmed that, in his view, my case was statute-barred. I had left it too late and, as I understood it, the case would be thrown out of court. I was very disappointed. But I was also determined to carry on if I could. Even if the case was never actually heard I knew it would be no comfort for Father Payne and the Church if it was thrown out on a legal technicality. I was encouraged by the last line in Tim O'Sullivan's letter: 'Kindly telephone this writer with your up-to-date instructions.' Surely there was an implication here that all was not yet lost? I telephoned him straight away.

'I've just received your letter setting out Gerard Durcan's opinion.'

'Well, as you can see, Mr Durcan is of the view that your case is statute-barred and he has set out the opinion in a detailed statement attached to the letter I sent you.'

'I was just wondering what my options were, if any. I thought from the last line of your letter that maybe there was still something I could do.'

'Well, it may be possible to initiate proceedings but you would have to understand that the chances of success are almost non-existent because at the end of the day your case is statute-barred and there's no way around that at the moment. The best we can do is write to Father Payne before issuing proceedings and see what happens after that.'

'Well, if that's still an option that's what I want to do.'

Tim O'Sullivan said he would have to go back to Gerard

Durcan and the whole procedure could take some time, but he would be in touch if there were any developments.

Over the next few months I worked my eighty-hour week and did my best to carry on as normal. Some of the people in the office spent a lot of money and time travelling in and out of work. I had a ten-minute walk. And while I got paid at the end of the month, I had my weekly wage from Bolebec House and the tips were good too. Most of the residents were extremely wealthy and looked after the porters well.

I had been able to buy some new clothes and my flat really felt like home. I kept it spotless and everything was in the same place all the time. All my perfectly pressed white shirts hung on individual hangers in a neat row in the wardrobe. Boxer shorts had a shelf of their own. Socks were folded facing outwards, ten black pairs, ten white pairs, always taken only from the right side. Tee-shirts were ironed to perfection and folded with precision. Everything had a place and was always put away. Even when I was going to bed the empty glass was washed and there were no clothes left lying around.

People found it strange that I had to have everything so perfect. Once, when Stephen was over from Dublin, he moved a few things a tiny bit while I was in the bathroom. A picture on the wall was shifted slightly so it wasn't hanging straight, the television was turned a couple of inches, a lampshade was tweaked and the bottle of scotch was not exactly where it was normally. I was back in the room only seconds before I picked out all the things he'd done. We laughed at the madness of it but I was always like that and it didn't bother me. I liked order in my life.

In March 1992 my solicitors told me that they had written to Father Payne.

Dear Sir,

We act for Mr Andrew Madden who is currently resident in England.

We are instructed by our client that during the period when our client was between the ages of 12 and 15 years, he suffered a series of sexual assaults perpetrated upon him by you. The said assaults have had a serious effect upon our client.

It is clear from our instructions that the said assaults are actionable and we therefore call upon you, within seven days of the date hereof, to formally admit liability and to furnish us with your written undertaking to compensate our client in full for damages and loss which he has sustained.

Failing hearing from you within the specified period, our instructions are to issue the appropriate proceedings against you without further notice.

We await hearing from you.

I was nervous and delighted. It sounded like my solicitors took everything as seriously as I did. They talked about 'said assaults have had a serious effect upon our client' and the 'loss which he has sustained', which made me feel that they cared. And indeed that they were now battling for me. 'Our client', the letter said. *Our client*.

But I was concerned for Father Payne. This letter was going to be a shock to him, even if it was one he deserved. I was worried about what he might do. I wanted my suffering acknowledged and those responsible brought to account, but a dead priest would bring about neither.

I had wanted to sue the Church but legal advice was that unless I could prove negligence by it, under current legislation I could only sue Father Payne. I wanted to avoid a situation where the Church could distance itself from him, claiming that apart from this one priest everything was fine. There had to be other Father Paynes and unlike Bishop O'Mahony I had no reason to believe that they might not be abusing other children. I also felt that the Church should be responsible for the actions of its priests. Health boards are responsible for nurses and doctors, education authorities responsible for teachers, the Home Office in London responsible for its police and prison wardens. Why should the Catholic Church in Ireland not be responsible for its priests?

The Church's lawyers, Arthur O'Hagan solicitors, replied in the middle of April:

> Dear Sirs,
> We act on behalf of Fr Ivan Payne who has consulted us in relation to your letter to him of 25th ult.
> We are presently taking more detailed instructions from our client.
> In the meantime strictly without prejudice we should be obliged if you would indicate the loss allegedly sustained by your client.
> Yours faithfully

Tim O'Sullivan wrote to me saying he had spoken to Father Payne's solicitor and his initial instructions were that I had already received certain payments from his client and could I give him details of such payments. *Payments?* The two hundred and fifty pounds due to Father Payne from eight years before when he had helped clear my drinking debts? But that was only one payment and the letter clearly said 'payments'. The only other money I had received was two pounds or thereabouts a week for 'gardening'. Did Father Payne really think I had been compensated for what had happened and the effects it had had on my life? I couldn't believe that he'd mentioned this to his solicitors. Had he no shame? I was furious that he seemed to be treating this so frivolously.

My solicitors recommended that I arrange to get a psychiatric opinion for use in the case. I had been to see my doctor several times over the last couple of years and he knew my past and was aware that I was often depressed. He arranged for me to see a psychiatrist, Dr Frank. I was worried about talking to a psychiatrist: most of my problems were still secret and other than telling my GP when I was very down, I had never spoken about anything in detail. I was with Dr Frank in his rooms near Harley Street for almost two hours. He asked lots of questions and wrote everything down. I told him as much as I could but it was difficult to put words on my feelings when I'd never really teased them out before. Dr Frank produced a general opinion based on this meeting which I sent to my solicitors. He concluded that the sexual abuse I had experienced as a child was a significant factor in my difficulties in adulthood.

He also recommended that I regulate my drinking – something I felt totally unable to do. I hadn't even told him the full extent of it or that drinking was the only thing which made me feel better about myself. Of course, I was pleased with how things were going at work and that I had a nice flat, but they didn't provide the contentment and consolation I got from a bottle of scotch.

Gerard Durcan suggested a meeting with Father Payne's solicitors. He thought the psychiatric report was very helpful but said that if the proposed meeting did not take place or was not fruitful we would need to give further and more detailed particulars of the effects the abuse had had. I was sorry I hadn't been able to speak more freely to Dr Frank but then it was difficult to talk so openly to someone I had just met.

In September my solicitors wrote to Arthur O'Hagan telling

them that we had a medical report ready and inviting them to meet us. In December they repeated the offer because the Church's solicitors still hadn't replied. Eventually a meeting was called at the Four Courts on 18 January 1993. I was looking forward to the meeting although I was also a little nervous. I knew Father Payne wouldn't be there so I wasn't worried about that, I was just anxious about what would happen. It was hard to imagine that the case would be resolved in just one meeting, but then why not? Father Payne and his solicitors had heard from my solicitors ten months earlier so they'd had plenty of time to consider what to do.

I wondered if Father Payne had told anyone – Archbishop Connell or Bishop O'Mahony or anyone else – that he was being sued for child abuse. I had no way of finding out. But I knew he was still working at the diocesan marriage tribunal at Archbishop's House, where people had to go about getting their marriages annulled, and he was still a chaplain at St Fintan's in Sutton. I kept tabs on his whereabouts by phoning both places regularly, pretending I wanted to send him a letter.

'Oh hello, I'm writing a confidential letter to Father Ivan Payne and I just wanted to make sure he is still at the marriage tribunal before I send it off.'

'Yes, he is. Can I ask who's calling, please?'

'No.'

The day of reckoning arrived. I hurried up O'Connell Street, not wanting to be late. It was so long since I'd been anywhere near the Four Courts I couldn't remember how far down the quays it was. I spotted Ken Duggan in the distance. I couldn't believe I would see him today of all days. I was in a hurry and he was with his family so I didn't call after him. Imagine him asking if I had any news! I'd track him down another day.

The huge round hallway of the courts building was buzzing with solicitors and barristers in wigs and gowns rushing from room to room, sometimes trailed by worried-looking clients. I was both anxious and excited. I'd met Tim O'Sullivan just once and could hardly remember what he looked like. He arrived and said he'd been talking to Gerard Durcan and that's why he was a bit late.

'I'll introduce you to Mr Durcan and he'll have a chat with you,' he said as we walked down a corridor. 'Then Mr Durcan and I will go and talk to Father Payne's solicitors, who are around here somewhere, while you wait in the room, and we'll get back to you as soon as we can. There's nothing to worry about – as I told you on the phone, Father Payne won't be here today.'

Gerard Durcan explained the procedure again and said that in the meeting with Arthur O'Hagan solicitors he would be showing them the medical report and would then put to them the amount of damages we were seeking. He said he found it very difficult to put a figure on damages because cases like this were rare in Ireland and he was sure that there had been no precedent involving the Church.

'What sort of a settlement would you consider, Andrew?'

I had given it some thought but would have liked guidance.

'Well, given all that's happened, and the fact that it went on for nearly three years, and given what Dr Frank said in his report – although it is only a very general report, and as you said yourself we might really need to give better and further particulars . . .'

I realized I was going on a bit and not answering his question.

'I think fifty thousand pounds would be a serious attempt on their part to show that they were acknowledging all that had happened, so I'll say fifty thousand.'

Tim O'Sullivan took notes.

'Well, as I say, it is very hard to put a value on the case,' Gerard Durcan said. 'I remember a case where a girl was assaulted once in a hospital and she was awarded twelve thousand pounds, so up against that fifty thousand pounds seems reasonable, but there are problems with the case – it is statute-barred after all – so we'll go and see what they have to say.'

They got up to leave the room.

'Is it okay if I smoke while I'm waiting?' I said.

'Smoke away,' said Tim O'Sullivan.

It seemed like they were gone for ages but it was less than half an hour before they returned.

'Right, we sought damages of seventy-five thousand pounds,' said Gerard Durcan. 'I don't think they were expecting that. They've had a look at the medical report and have asked for a second report to be done by someone of their own choosing. I've agreed to that and so they will write to Mr O'Sullivan with appointment details and he will be in touch with you. We have reminded them that you are living in London and they've accepted that the medical assessment will have to take place over there.'

'Will this go on for much longer?' I said.

'No. I'm sure we'll all be back here in the Four Courts in about three months' time.'

The meeting ended and we went our separate ways. I was furious. Father Payne's solicitors could have asked for their own medical report at any stage over the previous ten months. It had taken them nearly four months just to agree to meet us and now they were dragging their heels again. I went from wanting to protect Father Payne, if he had not gone on to abuse anyone else, to the other extreme. Even if I did win this case I might still go public about him, I thought – after all these years he was still messing me about, and if he had told the Church what was happening then it was doing the same.

I went home and phoned some newspapers. I needed an outlet for my anger but I also needed to be calm and controlled, so I was vague. I asked reporters whether they would be interested if I knew of someone suing a serving Catholic priest for child abuse, about which a member of the hierarchy had full knowledge. They definitely would, they all said, but they'd need much more information before they could publish anything. They wanted to meet me but I said no, not at the moment. Realizing how keen they were somehow calmed me down. It reminded me of how important it was to win this case and that I mustn't blow it out of anger and frustration.

Later that night, after I'd had plenty to drink, I told my sister Audrey and Pat, her husband, what I was doing. My friends Val and Stephen in Dublin knew all about the case, but this was the first anyone in my family had heard of it. They were shocked both at what I'd told them about 'things' – I left it at that – Father Payne had done to me and about the legal proceedings. I told them to say nothing to anyone. I returned to London and waited to hear from my solicitors.

# 11. Daniel

The months leading up to my trip to Dublin had been up and down. At the end of October I'd been to see my doctor again because my depression had become so bad and my nervousness, anxiety and panic attacks were too much to handle. He gave me thirteen weeks off work and put me on something that later became trendy – Prozac. I decided to stay on at Bolebec House. Though there were times when I found it difficult, it was my easiest job because I spent so much time on my own. I was afraid that if I stayed away from work altogether, my only contact with people would be in the Limelight on Monday nights when I'd be drinking, and that was hardly real life. It would be so much more difficult to go back to work having spent so much time alone.

The following Monday I went to the Limelight. It was boring because I knew no one there that night. When the lights came on at the end I noticed two guys standing at the end of the queue for the cloakroom. One was really good-looking and kept glancing in my direction. He smiled over and I smiled back. As I passed the queue he smiled again and I waited by the front door to see what would happen. Eventually he stood nearby with his friend. I knew that if I just walked out the door he would think I wasn't interested, and I really wanted to talk to him. As I stood almost in the doorway, I turned around and beckoned for him to come over to me.

'All right?' I asked.

'Hi, I'm Daniel.'

'I'm Andrew.'

'Where are you going now?'

'Em – home,' I said, not meaning to sound sarcastic.

'Oh yes, right, stupid question,' he said, and laughed.

He was so good-looking I just wanted him there and then. He was shorter than me, oriental, with a natural tan, dark hair, a beautiful smile of snow-white teeth and a great body.

'Which way are you going?' he said.

'I live in Pimlico.'

'Would you like a lift – I'm giving some other people a lift home as well – or if you want you can come back to my place?' He had a persuasive smile. It was obvious he was as keen as I was.

By the time he'd dropped off his friends we were nearer to his parents' house in Mill Hill than to my flat so we decided to go there. He said there would be no problem, his parents had relatives staying but he had his own room and a bathroom next door and his parents never came in.

We had a great night together. Daniel had a fabulous body and was much better built than me, but he didn't seem disappointed. In the morning he got up to shower, leaving me in bed. He closed the bedroom door behind him but a child – one of his relatives, I presumed – came into the room, took one look around and walked out, leaving the door open. Then I could hear a voice coming through the house, getting nearer, until a woman walked into the room. I couldn't make out what she was saying. Daniel had told me he was originally from Malaysia and I presumed this was his mother and she was speaking Malaysian. I pretended to be asleep. She was banging on Daniel's bathroom door shouting things at him. She needed Daniel's Renault because his father had taken the Mercedes to work so we'd have to get the Tube back in to central London and she was going to give us a lift to the station. I couldn't believe she was so casual after finding me in her son's bed. On the train Daniel explained that his mother knew he was gay but his father didn't. She knew he had boyfriends – he was nearly twenty-three, after all – so I didn't need to worry.

Daniel was meant to be going to college but came to my flat instead. I showered and we went back to bed. That evening he had to go home but we agreed to meet for lunch the following day in the Village in Soho. The Village was a gay café bar on the corner of Wardour Street and Brewer Street. I'd passed it before but was always afraid to go in. I arrived early and ordered a drink. I had to wear my navy suit, shirt and tie because I was due at Bolebec House at four o'clock but I was relaxed about it – I wasn't the only one in a suit. I sat near the window and watched for Daniel. Then I saw him across the road. He certainly stood out. He wore black jeans, a black top, a bright purple jacket and sunglasses and carried a rucksack over one shoulder. God, he looked gay.

We kissed and he sat down. He had an infectious personality and was a great talker. Though I thought he was gorgeous, I was uncomfortable because he wanted to keep holding my hand. I was just no good at constant shows of affection. And anyway affection was not something I felt for someone after a couple of days. We enjoyed lunch. Some of his friends came in and joined us for a while and then I had to leave. I gave Daniel the number for Bolebec House and he said he'd call me the next day.

The following evening at work I thought about him a lot. He'd phoned and I had said he could come to Bolebec House and stay with me in the office until my shift ended and then we could go back to my flat for the night. What was happening? If I kept seeing him it would be a relationship. He would be my boyfriend. I'd never had a boyfriend and I'd steered clear of relationships over the last three years. But I liked him too much not to see him again. Would he really want to know me if he knew about my problems? And what about the sex? Would I go off it as I seemed to with everyone else? Maybe it would be different with Daniel? I decided that when I saw him later I would have the answers: as soon as I set eyes on him, I would know what I wanted. A blue Mercedes pulled up in the drive and a smiling Daniel waved up at me. I opened the electric gates from the office. He parked in the basement and came up to reception in the lift.

'Hi, how are you?' he said.

'Oh, I'm fine, and you?' I said, staring into his eyes.

'I'm fine too. What's wrong? You're looking at me very strangely.'

'Nothing's wrong at all, I'm just thinking how nice you look.'

And that was it. I was hooked. He was gorgeous and he seemed to think I was as well. We stepped into the lift and kissed. I knew I was taking a chance but he was irresistible. I hoped neither of us would regret it.

Over the next few months we spent lots of time together and I was madly in love. Daniel spent most nights in my flat, which didn't please his parents. He had lots of friends on the gay scene and knew everyone. We never had to queue for the Limelight: Daniel knew the people who ran the gay night and we were permanently on the guest list. He bought two rings and asked me to wear one all the time to show people we were together. In December we went to Paris for three days to celebrate his birthday and visit a friend of his. We spent the mornings in bed, the afternoons sight-seeing and the nights in clubs, the best one being the famous Queen on the Champs-Elysées. We had our first row when Daniel walked into the bathroom while I was on the toilet and I shouted at him to get out. He seemed to think that because we were a couple nothing was private. I insisted there were things that not even couples did in front of each other, not least because they were hardly pleasant sights.

On Christmas Day he picked me up from Bolebec House after work and we had dinner with his parents and their other guests in Mill Hill. I had told Daniel about suing Father Payne, but I never mentioned how difficult things had been; he knew I was off work sick and that I was taking Prozac for depression but that was it. I didn't want him running away. In January he came to Dublin with me without telling his parents. I told my family he was a friend but I think my sister had her suspicions — not that anything was said. I was home for three weeks and Daniel stayed for just a few days. His parents were furious that he was spending so much time out of the house, and knew he wasn't studying as much as he should have been, so he couldn't stay the full three weeks. In a way I was glad. Although I loved him, I needed my own space. Especially when I was facing the meeting in the Four Courts which might have huge significance for the rest of my life.

## 12. Settlement

In February my solicitors wrote to Arthur O'Hagan solicitors reminding them that I was waiting for details of the psychiatric evaluation they were arranging for me. I was back at work and I was managing, but I was frustrated that Father Payne's lawyers were taking so long getting back to us. In April I wrote to Tim O'Sullivan saying that if I didn't get a date by 18 April I was withdrawing my consent for the second assessment. I had had enough. I was furious that so much time was passing and there seemed to be nothing I could do. This time I could not contain my anger so I wrote to Archbishop Connell (see Appendix).

I said it would be deplorable if he did not already know about my case, but in case he didn't, these were the details: Father Ivan Payne had abused me every week for three years when he was a chaplain at Christ The King parish in Cabra. Afterwards I had told a teacher and as a result Monsignor Alex Stenson, Bishop Dermot O'Mahony and some others in the Church became aware of my case. Father Payne was moved to Sutton. The abuse had hurt me badly and as a result a year previously I had initiated proceedings against Father Payne. 'I wanted justice,' I wrote, 'I wanted to seek an acknowledgement from the Church that I have suffered at the hands of Fr Payne and I wanted compensation.'

I explained my frustration at the delays and said that I had reached a point where I would be looking at every option open to me to get redress. 'Unless there is a radical change in some people's attitudes, which seems most unlikely, this matter is bound to move to the public domain,' I wrote. 'In such circumstances, I will not tolerate the Church authorities issuing statements to the effect that had they known about the proceedings pending against Fr Payne the whole matter would have been handled differently. I have now effectively closed that loophole because now, Archbishop, you do know.'

From a legal point of view, sending this letter was not a good idea. I was worried about what my solicitors would say. And I was telling Father Payne's employers that he was being sued and I wasn't sure that was allowed – would it be a breach of confidence or something? But I had to do something. I marked the envelope STRICTLY PRIVATE PERSONAL AND CONFIDENTIAL – DO NOT OPEN in the hope that the Archbishop would get to read it personally.

I expected to hear from Tim O'Sullivan fairly quickly. But instead within days I had a phone call from Archbishop's House. It was the man to whom Ken Duggan had taken my allegations twelve years earlier – Father Stenson then, now Monsignor Stenson, Chancellor of the Archdiocese of Dublin.

'Hello, Andrew, this is Alex Stenson here in Dublin.'

First names. Cosy.

'Good morning, Monsignor.'

'Andrew, I'm calling on behalf of His Grace, the Archbishop. He has received your letter and has asked me to tell you that the matter is receiving immediate attention. He also wanted me to tell you that he had no idea any of this was going on, but now I can assure you that everything will be dealt with immediately.'

'Okay, well thank you for getting back to me so quickly.'

'That's no problem and I will be confirming all of this in writing over the next couple of days. Just one other thing –

I've being talking to Bishop O'Mahony who said you came to see him a few years ago and he feels that maybe he should have stayed in contact with you. He feels he might have let you down because he was meant to get back to you and between one thing and another it never happened. He's asked me to pass on his number so if you ever want to talk to him, or indeed if you're in Dublin and you want to meet up with him, he'd be more than happy to see you.'

'I don't think that would be a very good idea at the moment with everything that's going on,' I said. 'I don't want him to think I'm being impolite or anything. I heard that he hadn't been too well and that his mother had died, so I thought maybe that's why he wasn't able to get back to me. And of course I moved back to London a few months after I last spoke to him, so there was that as well. So if you could tell him thanks for the offer and maybe I'll take it up at some stage in the future but I don't think now is a good time.'

'Okay, Andrew, I'll do that, and as I said I'll be writing to you over the next couple of days.'

He sounded friendly enough, which was probably the Archbishop's idea – I could just imagine him telling the Monsignor, 'For God's sake, be nice to him,' to make sure I didn't go running to the press or anyone else. I was delighted to have got such a direct response. I wondered if the Archbishop would call in the Church solicitors and Father Payne to ask them just what the heck had been going on behind his back for the last twelve months.

As promised, Monsignor Stenson confirmed what he had said in writing.

Some time later I got the letter I had been expecting from Tim O'Sullivan. He asked me to send him a copy of my letter to the Archbishop and advised me to 'desist from such correspondence at this time'. He said that Arthur O'Hagan solicitors had reconsidered the situation and no longer wanted to have me assessed by their own psychiatrist. I didn't need to ask what had brought about that change. Now they were talking to a barrister with a view to assessing the amount of damages payable to me, bearing in mind my difficulties due to statute of limitations. I was disgusted by that qualifier. I thought Father Payne and the Church should make a settlement based on three years of child abuse, not on the statute of limitations. However, they'd already shown themselves to be insensitive, to say the least, when it came to deciding the best thing to do, so I should not have been surprised.

In early June we were back in the Four Courts. I was pleased that Father Payne wouldn't be there; I still didn't want to meet him. Gerard Durcan said he didn't think the settlement would be anywhere near fifty thousand pounds and asked what was the least I would accept. I told him twenty thousand. If I accepted anything less I would be saying that really I hadn't been hurt in any serious way, and I wasn't prepared to do that. Anything less wouldn't be worth all of this; I'd rather have my day in court. Tim O'Sullivan and Gerard Durcan went to meet the Church lawyers and again I waited alone. They were gone for much longer than in January.

'Right, I've got twenty-seven and a half thousand,' Gerard Durcan said when they came back into the room.

I couldn't think of anything to say.

'Andrew, I strongly recommend you accept it. It's a lot of money and it's a good settlement.'

'Oh, I will accept it. It doesn't reflect everything but it is a lot of money and it does show that they've taken it seriously at last, so yes, I will accept it.'

My costs came to 15 per cent of the settlement – over four thousand pounds. The Church solicitors paid 10 per cent and both Tim O'Sullivan and Gerard Durcan agreed to waive the other 5 per cent. They said the 10 per cent covered their costs and they had no desire to make any money out of this particular case.

Gerard Durcan said the matter was now over, finished, and there was no going back. I agreed – thinking otherwise. There was no way I was keeping this to myself. Having my compensation was the proof that I had been abused. The media would take notice of such an amount and if I went public people would know I was telling the truth. As far as I knew it was the first time such a settlement had been reached in Ireland so the case was bigger than me. By now I was convinced that I couldn't be the only person ever abused by a priest and Father Payne couldn't be the only priest ever to abuse. If I could get compensation, however nominal, then so could other people and they needed to know that the precedent had been set. If this became public, people in similar situations would be encouraged to seek redress for their suffering – or at least tell someone about it and share their awful burden.

But I wasn't sure that I had the courage to go public. If I did, could I keep Father Payne's identity out of it? Maybe he hadn't abused anyone else and if he hadn't it seemed unfair to reveal his name. Still, I didn't know if I was the only one, and if I wasn't, if he made a habit of it, I couldn't very well keep his secret.

And there was one other issue: although I had no proof, I was sure the Church was involved in financing the settlement. There was so much stalling until my letter to the Archbishop. Then everything changed and in no time we had a settlement. I thought that was important too: it showed that the Church authorities were willing and able to bail out priests who admitted to having abused children – but only when threatened by court proceedings where names would be mentioned. I couldn't decide what to do. On days when I was particularly angry or depressed I would have told the world my story but on calmer days that didn't seem right. For now.

When my solicitors sent me the form of discharge to sign, it contained an admission of guilt, but no apology.

*I, Andrew Madden of 95 St George's Drive, Pimlico, London SW1V 4DB acknowledge receipt of the sum of £27,500 from Ivan Payne in full and final settlement of all claims howsoever or against whomsoever arising out of assaults upon me by the said Ivan Payne between the years 1977 and 1980 as set out in a letter dated 25 March 1992.*

I signed it on 17 June 1993.

## 13. No Drink, No Daniel

Daniel was now part of my life and I was more settled in a gay lifestyle and didn't mind people knowing I was gay; I didn't go out of my way to come out but in myself I felt fine about it. I was happier than I could ever remember because I knew how much Daniel loved me and I loved him. I had given up working Saturday and Sunday nights at Bolebec House to spend more time with him. On Saturdays he worked in Mulberry on Beauchamp Place. Usually I drove him to work and picked him up in the evening. I would watch as he walked down the street looking for me and see his face light up when he spotted the car. At those moments it always struck me just how much I loved him: I adored the very sight of him. Of course, there were other good times too, but this was different, private, special – a chance for me to observe him secretly and savour the feelings of love.

But I wasn't very good at showing love. Already I had lost interest in physical intimacy; we still had sex but not as often as Daniel wanted. One Friday night he went to a club with friends and I went to bed alone thinking he was just staying out particularly late. In the morning he came into the flat on his way to work. I was still in bed and he kissed me.

'Sorry I didn't make it home last night.'

'What happened?'

'I had too much to drink, left the car in town and Birrol drove me home instead. Anyway, I have to rush, I'm already late for work. Will you meet me for lunch?'

'Okay, I'll ring you later and we can arrange a time.'

I lay in bed and began to think. He liked a drink but usually never drank too much. And if he was that drunk, why did he go home to his parents? And if Birrol was driving him, why go all the way to Mill Hill when my flat was so much nearer, especially when he was working the next day? It didn't add up. Obviously he had something to hide and it didn't take much to work out what.

Over lunch I asked and he couldn't answer. He smiled and looked like a little boy who knew he was in trouble. He admitted he'd spent the night with someone else. I loved him too much to be really angry. Anyway, it was partly my fault: if I couldn't give him as much sex as he needed then he had to get it somewhere else. I valued his love more than his body and I knew that in that regard he was exclusively mine. I was afraid he would leave me if I told him not to do it again so I said I wasn't too upset. I said he could do it again if he had to as long as it was just a one-night stand; two or three nights might become a relationship and I wasn't having that. And he wasn't to sleep with any of our friends.

Later he threw this back at me, saying I couldn't really love him if I didn't mind him sleeping with other people. He couldn't see that it was because I loved him so much that I didn't mind. He was young and only human and it was natural for him to need more than I could offer. I was just pleased that he still found me attractive. There were plenty of better-looking guys in the Limelight. I was so skinny that they couldn't but have better bodies.

In so many ways, it seemed, I made Daniel think I didn't love him. Not wanting sex as much as he did meant he was always looking for ways to test me. I always went home at lunch-time to watch the news and *Neighbours* and have a scotch and coke. Sometimes Daniel would be in the flat if he'd finished college early, or not gone in at all. Rather than be happy that we were there together he wanted to hold hands while we sat on the bed watching television. Or he'd try to hold my hand as he drove along. It just wasn't — isn't — me: I'm not a tactile hand-holding type. But when we rowed this was evidence that I didn't really love him: it was just *his* hand I didn't want to hold.

It was the same in bed. I can't lie there holding someone all night. I don't mind for a few minutes but then I need to turn over and go to sleep. More rejection, he thought.

There were nights when he would put his arms around me and then move one hand down to my genitals. I hated that: it was too much like what Father Payne used to do. Daniel knew about Father Payne, but I couldn't tell him that when he touched me in that way it reminded me of being abused. How can you say that to someone you're supposed to love and expect them to stay?

After one really bad row we didn't see each other for a few days. Daniel phoned from his bedroom in Mill Hill. He said he was sad that the relationship wasn't working out. He said that as he talked he was taking tablets. Then his father walked into the room and Daniel put the phone down. A few minutes later his mother phoned to say that his father had taken him to the hospital to make sure he was all right. She asked me not to leave Daniel, at least not until after his exams. She reminded me that he was their only child and their lives would be ruined if anything happened to him. I told her I had no intention of leaving him, we were just going through a bad patch. I couldn't believe the emotional blackmail but decided to let it pass: she was the mother-in-law after all. I spent that night at Daniel's house. We vowed never to leave each other.

The good times together far outweighed the bad. Daniel had a great influence over me. Being loved by him really raised my self-esteem, made me feel worthwhile. And he showed me a different side of life. He proved that you didn't need money to have style – just well-off parents and the use of a Mercedes. Before we met I would never go into the exclusive shops around Knightsbridge. Daniel changed all that. Everything he owned had a designer label: Armani jeans, Rayban sunglasses, a Mulberry diary, a Cartier watch. I bought the same, minus the three-thousand-pound watch. The best present I bought him was a coveted Louis Vuitton rucksack which cost nearly five hundred pounds. Five hundred pounds for a rucksack – I really was madly in love. He introduced me to the exclusive Montpeliano and San Lorenzo restaurants. I paid the bills. Before we met I was thinking of buying a Ford Escort. Now I wouldn't even look at a car unless it was German. I still won't. Only the best for the boy with no money.

Daniel wasn't doing well at the London School of Economics and failed some of his exams. He was doing business studies because it was what his parents wanted. He was far more suited to something more flamboyant and creative, like fashion or interior design. I didn't care as long as he was happy. He left the LSE and continued his studies at Royal Holloway College in Surrey. He didn't have too many classes to attend and although he had student accommodation he came back to London most nights and every weekend. I used to worry about him driving so much, it increased the chances of an accident.

In November we went to Kinky Gerlinky for the second time. Kinky Gerlinky was a huge drag show held at the Empire in Leicester Square. Daniel wasn't a transvestite but for Kinky Gerlinky he'd dress up for fun. 'I Will Always Love You' was our song, so the first time he went as Whitney Houston. He looked great but I couldn't wait until we got home and he changed back to himself. I'd missed him. In November he went as Claudia Schiffer. Daniel knew there was no way I was dressing up but promised I'd get in anyway. When we got there the area in front of the Empire was cordoned off. Hundreds of people had gathered to watch all the stilettos, sling-backs and bouffants. The bouncers wouldn't let me in and Daniel had to go in and fetch the hostess, Naomi Campbell look-alike Winston, who swanned out in a flurry of yellow and plucked me from the crowd.

Soon afterwards Daniel was unfaithful with an ex-boyfriend of his. I was more upset this time and it led to a huge row. We didn't see each other for two weeks and then I phoned him on his mobile on Christmas Eve night. I was working at Bolebec House and he was nearby having dinner with his parents at the Hilton Hotel. I missed him dreadfully and he said he missed me too. I was staying at Bolebec House that night because I was back on duty at eight on Christmas morning. Daniel arrived shortly after 1 a.m. 'Don't ever let me leave you again,' he said. I gave him his Christmas present. He hadn't bought me anything but I didn't care; he was back.

Soon we were in trouble again, however Daniel told me he was going to Oxford for the weekend to meet Edith, a friend who had moved over from Paris. He said I probably wouldn't enjoy it because there would be lots of people: he knew I could be uneasy in large groups. He stayed with me on Thursday night. I told him I wanted him to have a good time and that yes, I would miss him – I loved our weekends together – but it was just one weekend so he wasn't to worry about me. We hugged and kissed and I told him again how much I loved him.

Late on Sunday night he came back to the flat wearing a cravat.

'Edith must be missing Paris,' I said.

'How do you mean?'

'She's got you wearing a cravat.'

'Oh that, no, I was just cold.'

I poured us a drink and afterwards we drove to Surrey for the night because he had an early class in the morning. As we lay on his bed watching television I took off the cravat. His neck was covered in bruises.

'What the hell's happened here?'

Daniel was half-smiling.

'Well? When did this happen? You met someone when you were out with Edith, didn't you?'

Daniel didn't answer.

'Were you with Edith at all over the weekend?'

Still no reply.

'You weren't, were you? You spent the whole weekend with someone else, didn't you? You'd no intention of going to see her at all. So where were you? Come on, who is he?'

'Someone I met in college,' said Daniel, not looking too worried.

'Here in Holloway?'

'No, he's at UMIST in Manchester.'

'So how the hell did you meet him in Surrey?'

'Through the computer in my class, we sent each other messages.'

'*We sent each other messages?* You left me thinking you were spending the weekend with Edith and really you'd planned a weekend away with some guy you met on the fucking computer?'

One of the other students knocked on the door and asked us to keep it quiet. It was after two in the morning. I couldn't speak to Daniel for ages and then I asked the guy's name.

'George.'

'George? It's not Boy fucking George by any chance?

You're not jealous because I'm a fan of his and decided to go and sleep with him just to get back at me?'

The idea of Daniel sleeping with my hero was too stupid for words and we both ended up laughing, but still not talking. We went to bed. Daniel initiated the sex and I was deliberately rough.

The following day the shock really hit me. I refused to speak to Daniel. It wasn't that he'd had sex with someone else, it was the calculation and the lies that really hurt. I couldn't believe he'd listened to me telling him how much I'd miss him and how much I loved him, all the time thinking about someone else. I felt sick. It would be a while before I could forgive this.

That afternoon we drove to Pimlico in silence. I watched television and drank a large scotch; Daniel read his book. While I cooked dinner he went downstairs to use the pay-phone in the hall to call his mother. He was gone for ages and the dinner started burning. I tiptoed down the stairs until I could hear his voice. He wasn't talking to his mother.

'Of course I love you, you know I do. We've just spent the weekend together and I'm coming back up to see you tomorrow. No, don't worry. We sleep in the same bed but we never have sex any more. Look, I'll have to go – phone me at eleven and we'll talk some more.'

I made it back to the kitchen without Daniel realizing I'd been listening.

'My mother's calling me back at eleven o'clock,' he said.

'No, she's not.'

'What do you mean, she's not?'

'I went down to get you because the dinner was burning and I heard everything: George is phoning you back at eleven, not your mother.'

'Well, they're both phoning back.'

He couldn't bring himself to look at me so he didn't see the tears in my eyes. We hardly said another word that night. I was livid and at the same time sick with hurt. I should have fought for him but I couldn't even speak to him.

The following day was no better. I went to Hyde Park for a long walk and when I came back he'd packed his things.

'I'm off now.'

'Are you really going to him?'

'Yes.'

I couldn't bear to look at him.

'Don't do anything I wouldn't do,' he said as he left to start his new life with gorgeous George.


For weeks I was useless. I drank even more than usual and became terribly depressed. I played my music and cried my eyes out. I'd been promoted to executive officer at the LCD and this time I had taken up the position. My job was in the Public Trust Office. Eventually I couldn't face work any more and just went out sick. I wanted to die. Daniel didn't phone and I didn't want to phone him. I expected him to come back but it became obvious that he wasn't going to.

My GP told me drinking was making everything worse. Several times he recommended that I stop but I didn't think I could. Drink was the only comfort I had. Eventually I agreed to give it a try: I felt so bad that I had to do something. I told him I would have to do it as an in-patient.

I had been drinking almost every day since that weekend in Ballycreen over ten years earlier and the idea that as soon as there was a bed available for me over the next few days I would stop drinking seemed impossible. My doctor wanted me to go to the Rugby House Clinic in Russell Square. He sent in my details and told me to phone the clinic every day to see if a place had come up.

I got home to find a letter from the finance company saying that I still owed them nearly three and a half thousand pounds but if I could make a one-off payment of just under two thousand pounds then my debt would be cleared. I sent the cheque. I'd always thought that if you did something good it would come back to you: that day I thought God was sending a message that giving up drink was the right thing to do. I carried on drinking knowing I only had a few days of it left.

Daniel phoned me at Bolebec House. It was good to hear his voice but I was disappointed when he said he was staying in Manchester. He was just phoning to find out if I was okay. I told him my news. He wasn't that impressed. My drinking had never been a problem in our relationship because I could drink so much without getting drunk. It didn't cause arguments and it didn't get in the way of whatever sex life we did have. He only ever worried about it as a health issue. It didn't stop him joining me, though his measures were small and one drink lasted him ages.

One morning when I phoned the clinic a place had become available. 'Be here by twelve o'clock and don't have anything to drink before you come,' I was told. I phoned the head porter at Bolebec House to say I wouldn't be coming to work. Before leaving the flat I looked at all the bottles in the corner of the room. I still had some I'd been given at Christmas – wine, champagne, vodka, gin and, of course, scotch. I nearly cried. I sat in the back of the cab, my heart racing. I had told my family what I was doing and they were pleased and relieved. My father had offered to come to London but I told him I'd get all the help I needed at the clinic. Really I wanted Daniel, but there was no sign of him. I couldn't believe he wasn't there for me, helping me through it. I felt so lonely – no alcohol and no Daniel, the two things I loved the most were gone. I couldn't believe I would not have a drink that night.

I was shown to a bedroom with two single beds and a small sink. A staff member asked me about my drinking and explained the routine. There were thirteen residents staying at the clinic, most of whom stayed for the full twenty-eight-day course. I said I would be staying for just a week: if I got through a full week without a drink I would be so amazed I was sure I'd be all right after that. There was a mandatory group meeting every day at two o'clock and every second day there was a one-to-one meeting with one of the staff. You had to be up by ten in the morning and in bed by two. For the first two days I wouldn't be allowed out – if I needed anything from the shop someone else had to get it.

I decided to give up smoking too. I smoked twenty a day and knew that if I didn't give up cigarettes when I was giving up drink I would soon be on eighty a day through comfort smoking. There was no point giving up drink only to die of lung cancer.

As the time for my first group meeting came closer, the lounge filled up. Everyone smoked non-stop.

'Are you one of us or one of them?' I was asked.

'How do you mean?'

'Are you a new member of staff or are you staying here?'

'Oh, I'm staying here.'

Three of the others were Irish and most of us were in our twenties or thirties. They had thought I was staff because they were all really sick when they arrived – looking awful, shaking, vomiting, unable to eat or sleep, always trying to get more medication than allowed. One or two of them were confined to bed. By that standard, I seemed fine.

When I went to my room to wait for the doctor that evening I discovered I had a new room-mate. He looked about forty but he was probably much younger. His face was covered in dried blood and he was filthy and he made the room stink. I guessed he might be homeless. I tried chatting but he didn't want to. I said I was waiting for the doctor and he asked what medication I was on. I said nothing yet – it was my first day. He told me to ask the doctor for some extra Tamazepan pills. The doctor would watch me put it in my mouth but I was to leave it under my tongue and give it to him afterwards. I said I wouldn't have the nerve and it was bound to go all wrong. He wasn't too happy.

I was feeling awful. It was tea-time and if I'd been in my nice warm flat, I'd be lying on the bed, watching television and sipping a scotch and coke. Instead I was in this dreary clinic full of people I didn't know and probably about to be mugged by my new room-mate.

I told the doctor I was feeling very depressed. I told him about Father Payne, about missing Daniel and about how desperately I wanted a drink. He put me on Librium and said the staff would give me the tablets at regular intervals. I stayed up watching television until two.

The following day I was exhausted and ratty. My room-mate had snored heavily all night long and I hadn't slept, but he was telling everyone I'd kept him awake all night with my snoring. I wanted to punch him. Apart from the snoring his smell made me sick. But I didn't want to complain about him – if he was trying to sort himself out it wouldn't have been fair. I just wished he'd shut the fuck up. Magnus from Bolebec House phoned to ask how I was which was a nice surprise. I was pleased with myself that I'd come through the first day. A day without alcohol for the first time in years. I thought about Daniel all the time: imagine if he paid me a surprise visit – that would make the day so much easier.

Everyone found a replacement for drinking. Most people

smoked more than usual. Others drank tea or coffee constantly. One girl went through dozens of cans of coke. I drank orange squash and ate digestive biscuits all day. Sleeping was no easier the second night. I got up at six o'clock and asked one of the staff to come and listen to the snoring. She didn't even have to come into the room, he was that loud. He spent the morning complaining about me again. One of the other residents was leaving that day and I was allowed to move rooms.

After the group meeting I had my one-to-one because I said I was going out for the day. Having been so depressed in recent weeks, I hadn't bothered to keep my flat in its usual impeccable order and I wanted to spend the evening cleaning and polishing. They were reluctant to let me go because the flat had been my main drinking environment. But I knew I wasn't going to drink. I'd had an amazing two full days without alcohol and I felt strong.

It was Saturday and I knew Daniel would be working. I desperately wanted to see him. I took a cab to Knightsbridge and called in to Mulberry. He looked as fabulous as ever.

'Well, hello, how are you?' he said, all smiles.

'I'm fine. Are you due for a break?'

'I could take a break now, do you want to go for coffee or something?'

We dodged the traffic on the Brompton Road to get to the Montpeliano Café. I had coke and Daniel had a cappuccino. I felt very relaxed – the Librium, I guessed.

'So what's happening – have you been to that place yet?' he said.

'Rugby House, yes, this is my third day. You're allowed out after two days but you have to be in by eleven at night. They breathalyse you and throw you out if you've had a drink.'

I started to tell him about it but I got the impression he was bored. I don't think he had any idea of the enormity of what I was doing. He wanted to talk about other things, so I listened; at least he was keen to talk to me. Maybe we could be best friends. My feelings were mixed. I was delighted to be with him, I hadn't seen him for so long, but I was conscious that time was short.

'I'll be in the flat until about half past nine if you want to drop in,' I said.

'Can't. I'm having dinner with my parents, then I'm seeing . . . you know.'

'Oh, he's down, is he?'

My heart sank.

'Will I ring you next week? If you don't want me to I'll understand,' he said.

'Well, after I come out of Rugby House I'm going to Dublin for five days – it wouldn't be good to spend too much time alone straight after I come out – but when I come back you can give me a ring.'

We said our goodbyes and I went to the flat. I kept thinking about drink. I put all the bottles – some full, some half-empty – in a plastic bag and threw them into the large bin the council kept across the road. Some poor scavenger was in for a nice surprise. I scrubbed and hoovered and polished and returned the flat to its normal pristine state. I left clothes at the laundry. I bought flowers for a vase Daniel had given me. I kept it on the mantelpiece beside a picture of him taken in his home town of Penang.

When everything was perfect I watched television for a while. It was strange not having a drink beside me. I wondered about non-alcoholic lager. Surely I could drink that? At least then I would feel like I was drinking. I phoned Rugby House for an opinion.

'Absolutely not. Maybe after a while, but on day three it wouldn't be a good idea,' said a worried member of staff.

I went down to the shop and bought coke and decided to try Pringles. People were always going on about the sour-cream Pringles and I needed to get a buzz out of something. I made my way back to the clinic and passed the breathalyser test.

On the eighth day I left Rugby House to fly to Ireland: the thought of spending Easter alone – no drink, no Daniel – was too much. I had to get away. Back in Dublin everyone said I looked very well. But they always said that. Still, I felt good that so much time – eight days – had passed since my last drink. I just wished I could sleep better. I was off the medication and the staff had said I had no physical need to drink any more. From now on it would all be psychological.

After Easter I returned to work in Bolebec House. It was great to be back and every day I was that little bit more proud of myself. I attended a weekly relapse prevention course at a substance abuse treatment centre in Hammersmith and I spent an hour every week talking to Dr Robert Cohen, who was assigned to give me one-to-one support. Over the summer months he listened to me talking about coping without alcohol. He knew I was still hurting badly over Daniel and advised against continuing the friendship, but I needed it. He also advised against starting counselling for the child abuse because he felt talking about the past could easily be a trigger for going back to drink.

I was accepted back into the LCD but I forfeited my promotion again. The stress and anxiety I used to feel in the office eased considerably and I felt more confident. I had more money than ever because I wasn't drinking. I felt healthier and ate more than I used to, though I hardly put on any weight.

I kept a note in my diary of how long it had been since my

last drink – eight weeks four days, twelve weeks six days, and so on. I kept telling myself I could do it. I was strong, I'd already proved how strong I was, and this raised my confidence to some extent.

But there was also a down-side to my new life. My flat became unbearable: I could no longer stay in and relax watching television or playing music. I had to be out all the time. It was easier to sit in cafés and bars in Soho, surrounded by people drinking, than it was to stay at home, because my flat had been my drinking environment. And the nervousness that came with being with so many people never went away. Not having Daniel to rely on, I had to find my own way around the gay scene. Only one of his friends kept in touch but he didn't go out much. The others told Daniel that all the time I was going out with him I was making passes at them. *As if.* I was still so tense that I never ordered tea or coffee and rarely held a glass. I drank small bottles of water. A bottle was always easier to hold. 'I don't need a glass, I'll have it out of the bottle,' I used to say.

I still couldn't talk to anyone. I nearly always left it to them to approach me first. And I turned down anyone who made a move. Without a drink I didn't feel able to bring someone back to the flat. I tried a couple of times and the sex was boring: I didn't feel confident about my body and just wanted to get it over with.

The only good sex I had was with Daniel when he was being unfaithful to gorgeous George. We had two great nights together early in the summer and both times the sex was initiated by him. I loved it. I loved being with him. Those two nights re-created the passion of the early part of the relationship. But Daniel was only using me because he was feeling rampant. The next time I tried to have sex with him he turned me away: 'I'm not used to having sex with

my friends.' It hadn't stopped him when he was going out
with me.

Our friendship was based on me chasing Daniel, phoning
him, making arrangements to meet up. The only time he
sought me out was when he passed Bolebec House on his way
from work to his parents – and that was only because he knew
I'd see him drive past. I begged him to come back. I wrote a
pleading letter. But George was nineteen, well-built and very
good-looking, and probably doing well at college. How could
I – anxious, depressed, skinny – compete? The only thing I
had that he didn't was money.

'How many people do we know who are still going out
with the people they were going out with when they were
nineteen?' I asked Daniel. 'Not a single one, is there? You had
me for life and you left me for a nineteen-year-old. How long
do you think that's going to last?'

Nothing worked. If anything, things got worse. If we had
arranged to meet, Daniel either turned up hours late or not at
all. He promised to come to the flat one Saturday night at
about eleven after dinner with his parents. He turned up two
hours later saying he'd called in to a friend who was managing
a restaurant in Pimlico, and he'd lost track of time. Fifteen
minutes later he had to go to a public phone box to call
George in Manchester. He didn't come back for two hours. I
was livid. It wasn't as if I could relax with a couple of drinks
while waiting – I just paced up and down the flat. Eventually
I had to sit outside and watch for him because I couldn't bear
to be inside. I lost my temper when he came back. We had
been the most important person in each other's lives and now
he was treating me like shit. He said sorry. But he always said
sorry. He threatened to go back to Mill Hill if I didn't stop
moaning. Despite my broken heart I gave in.

A couple of weeks later it happened again. He was moving

to Manchester to be with George and I was going with him for a Sunday afternoon's shopping in Habitat and the Reject Shop on the King's Road. He was supposed to pick me up at two but arrived closer to five. We just about made it before closing time. Shopping with Daniel in the Reject Shop. How appropriate, I thought.

## 14. Leaving London

At the end of September 1994 I went to Dublin to celebrate my birthday with Audrey. There was a surprise party for us at the Hole in the Wall. Helen, my friend from the LCD, and her boyfriend flew in for the party. I spent the night worrying that someone might have arranged a stripogram. If I'd been drinking I wouldn't have been worried – I would have laughed it off – but sober, and surrounded by so many people, I really would be the centre of attention. Fear ruined the night.

I had believed giving up drink would help my problems. I thought my chronic anxiety would go away but it didn't. In nearly eight months I'd only had decent sex twice. And the fun I used to have in clubs was all gone. Now I went only to get out of the flat and when I got there I was often on my own all night – too self-conscious to dance and somehow angry at anyone who showed an interest in me. And it was obvious. *Try and look like you're enjoying yourself* or *Penny for them* or *Smile, it might never happen*, people would say. I'd walk all the way back to Pimlico just to pass the early hours. I had some friends who didn't drink much, but at least they could when they wanted. Anyway, they oozed confidence without it.

I still got depressed but not as often. Sometimes people told me I looked wrecked. I had bags under my eyes from lack of sleep. I'd hardly cried since I stopped drinking. I just didn't feel anything. At least when I was drinking I let it out when things were really bad and then felt the better for it. I was fed up with the raw deal.

I desperately wanted to drink again. Everyone else was having fun and I had become a complete bore. I had no outlet for stress. So while I might avoid dying of liver disease a heart attack would probably get me instead. I started smoking again. I'd been to another alcoholics' relapse prevention programme but I couldn't relate to the other people's stories: the sorts of lives they'd had while drinking didn't sound anything like mine. I cried my eyes out at the last meeting before I'd come home. I was so disappointed that life without alcohol was such a let-down. Although I wanted to drink again I didn't want to drink the quantities I had before. The prospect of that had me scared. But I hoped I could handle drinking. Having gone without a drink for so long was surely proof that if I started again I wouldn't need it as much as I had before and I would be in control.

On the flight back to London, after six months, three weeks and five days of abstinence, I had two scotches. The familiar taste was exhilarating. I felt guilty but I'd thought it through and this was what I wanted. I put negative feelings to the back of my mind. On the way to my flat I stopped at an off-licence and bought a bottle of scotch. After unpacking I relaxed in front of the television with another few drinks. The measures were small but, not having had any alcohol for so long, it went straight to my head. I phoned a guy who had fancied me for ages and invited him round. Before, I would have been embarrassed being in bed with him, he had such a good body. Now I didn't care, I'd lost my inhibitions and I felt good.

Over the next few days I made a point of not having a drink. Then I starting drinking lager, although it took a while to find one I liked. That way I could cut down on the scotch by just having a couple at the end of the night.

Within weeks my depression was the worst it had ever been. Things had not been going well in the LCD. On top of my own work I had to train a new boss. She'd had a two-week introductory session but I was responsible for her on-the-job training. I didn't mind – I'd done it before with others – but we didn't get on well and it made work more difficult at a time when I just didn't need any difficulties.

I saw hardly anything of Daniel and still missed him terribly. I was no more over him than the day he'd left. He was treating me like something he couldn't wipe off the sole of his shoe and I felt worthless. He who had once loved me so much didn't care for me at all. I was humiliated by his indifference to my efforts to be friends. Even little things hurt dreadfully. Like when he called for me one evening, when I had arranged for us to go out together, and I had to sit in the back of his car because he'd brought another friend of his along and he was sitting in the front passenger seat. I'd never had to do that before. I might as well have been in the boot for all he cared.

I was so depressed that small setbacks were devastating. I had four designer key rings together on a bunch of keys – all expensive presents from Daniel. Their real value was that they were from him. I left them in the back of a cab one night and couldn't get them back. It was like another little bit of him had gone.

I stopped going into work. I went to talk to Dr Cohen nearly every day and I went back to working a five-night week at Bolebec House. I didn't need free weekends any more. The rest of the time I stayed in the flat. But even Bolebec House had become difficult: Magnus had become very pally with one of the residents and spent a lot of time hanging around instead of going home after his shift. One of the things I had liked about the job was that it was just me and the residents. It was my shift and I was in control and most of the time I could cope. Now he was hanging around with his friends and I might as well have been trapped in an office at the centre of attention I dreaded.

To escape the depression I started drinking heavily again, but I just became more depressed than ever. I'd been suicidal in the past but this was worse. I hated to wake up: I hated to be still alive. I remembered my first night in the flat when I lay in bed and looked around feeling really good about everything. Now I didn't want to take my head out from under the duvet. I'd keep my eyes closed, hoping I'd fall asleep again and escape a few hours of the long day.

I didn't want to spend the rest of my life like this but I couldn't see it getting better. And I might have forty years ahead of me even if I kept drinking. The blood tests I'd had when I stopped showed that there was virtually no damage to my system after all those years. I had a shortage of red or white blood cells – I couldn't remember which – but even that righted itself after three months of abstinence. So there was no way the alcohol would finish me off quickly. I went to a few pharmacies and accumulated about 150 paracetamol tablets. I knew if I took them on their own I could take days to die and, contrary to popular belief, I would be conscious the whole time, dying slowly from internal bleeding. I planned to fill my blender with scotch, pills, cream and maybe fruit to make the whole thing more palatable. If I added scotch, and if I could drink the whole thing down quickly, it would probably knock me out.

I wasn't about to kill myself straight away but I wanted to have everything ready so that I could do it whenever I wanted. I cried at the prospect of what I was doing. I knew my friends would be upset but they'd get over it. My family would be ruined but even that thought didn't put me off. In my diary I had named Daniel as the contact in the event of an emergency. I didn't want him being told of my death over the phone –

the thought of him running through Manchester, looking for George, panicking and crying made me feel terrible – so I put down his parents' names instead. They could tell him in person.

I was in this state, actively planning my death, for about twelve days. Dr Cohen phoned to say I'd missed an appointment. I went to see him and told him how things were. He said I was clinically suicidal and wanted me to go into hospital. I refused. In a perverse sort of way I was all right: though it felt awful, I was in control. It was totally in my hands whether I came through this or not and I wanted it to stay that way. He was worried about letting me home and told me he wanted to see me first thing on Monday morning at the hospital. He said he might use his powers under the Mental Health Act to force me into hospital if he still thought I needed it and I wouldn't agree to admit myself. I said that though I was struggling at Bolebec House, it was my only remaining link with normality, and if I gave that up and went into hospital, for what could be a long time, I might never work again.

That evening the welfare officer from the LCD came to see me at the flat. I sat on my bed in tears as I told her everything. She was afraid to leave. She asked me to give her the paracetamol. I said there was no point, I could just go and buy more. She suggested entering into a pact, asking me to make a solemn promise not to do anything over the weekend, to at least try to hang on until Monday morning's appointment with Dr Cohen. I told her it was a waste of time but accepted her home phone number. That night I stayed in, having told Magnus I was sick and wasn't coming to work.

And that was the last day of it.

Saturday morning I felt a little better. I was still feeling down, feeling sad, but I knew I wasn't going to kill myself. I went to Bolebec House and work went okay. I phoned the welfare officer from the LCD and told her of the improvement; I didn't want to ruin her weekend. I didn't have a home number for Dr Cohen. That night I went to GAY on Charing Cross Road, the biggest and best club on a Saturday night. My friends Sudesh, Mohammed and Dennis were there. I felt so much better being out again. Though it had only been a few weeks, it felt like I hadn't been out for months. They had been long, dark weeks.

I don't know how I came through those twelve days. I think knowing that I could end it all at any time comforted me: I wasn't going to have to feel so bad for years to come because I could end the pain whenever I wanted. Also, I think the prospect of being forced into hospital shocked me and something in me started fighting back. Dr Cohen probably saw that and that's why he took a chance and allowed me home. If I was wanting to go to Bolebec House, and talking about being afraid that I would never work again if I didn't, obviously a part of me was struggling to keep going.

I went out several nights a week for the next couple of months – Fridays at the Phoenix in Cavendish Square, Saturdays at GAY, Sundays at the LYC, and back to GAY on Mondays. I finished work at midnight, went home to shower and change and was in the clubs shortly after one o'clock. I was resigned to the fact that Daniel's relationship with George was going well – they'd been together for eight or nine months. I was lonely and enjoyed the escapism of club life. I met lots of guys and slept with most of them just the once. They were nearly all orientals like Daniel, though I had my share of black guys as well. What they say is true.

Shortly before Christmas Daniel got in touch. We a to meet up at the Phoenix at about eleven o'clock I had a few drinks with Sonia who lived in th We regularly got together to swap stor arrived shortly after ten o'clock and drove us to the club in his Yugo.

I was excited about seeing Daniel but angry that he'd let so much time pass – about two months – without being in touch. Instead of calling in to see me in Bolebec House when he was passing, now he drove on with his friends. The first time it happened I phoned him later and started shouting and he put the phone down on me. I called straight back and his mother answered, saying Daniel was busy having his dinner. I was furious with her. She didn't mind phoning me when Daniel was upset but when I was upset he wasn't to be disturbed from his dinner.

He arrived at the Phoenix with a friend from college two hours later than agreed. He was in jeans, boots, a beige sweat-shirt and a red baseball cap. I couldn't take my eyes off him. I wanted him so much. I drank too much and started getting upset. I stood at the bar watching him dance and couldn't cope with the sadness. Eventually I went outside and sat in the rain drinking from two bottles of Budweiser.

The club ended at three o'clock and people started coming out on to the street. Daniel came out and tried to talk to me but I just started shouting at him. The Mercedes was parked right outside the club and he started to drive away saying he'd phone me during the week. I didn't want him to go. I smashed one of the bottles on to the pavement near the car. Then I stood in front of the car so he couldn't move. He got out and tried reasoning with me but I was having none of it. I cried and shouted at him. I raved about his two-timing, his creeping off with George, his empty promises to stay friends but leaving all the running to me. When I'd got it all out I let him go. About a hundred people were standing on the pavement looking at me and I just walked away. Dennis caught up with took me home.

The next day I sent Daniel the biggest bunch of flowers I could persuade Interflora to make up. I couldn't bear the thought that he might never speak to me again. A day later I phoned him and apologized. He said he was going to phone but thought I must really hate him. I said the problem was I still loved him so much.

A few weeks later he was down in London. When he was going back to Manchester I said I wanted to go with him. We'd got on so well I didn't want our time together to end.

'What about George? I don't want any trouble between you two,' he said.

I'd spoken to George just once, when I'd answered Daniel's mobile phone. Months earlier I'd wanted to rip his head off but now we were quite civil to each other.

'I'll be fine if he's fine. I'll stay in a hotel nearby and the three of us can meet up when you're finished at college and just go out and have a good time.'

Daniel cleared it with George. He was worried about flying Budweiser bottles. Daniel told him that had been a one-off. I shook hands with gorgeous George who was waiting for us on the station platform. He certainly lived up to the nickname I'd bestowed. They said I should stay in their flat for that night at least. It was small but nice. The bedroom was just an extension of the living-room with a wardrobe to block it off. With me on the couch we would really be sleeping in the same room. I hoped they weren't planning on sex, I couldn't have handled that. We stayed up late talking. In the morning they left for college and I headed for the hotel. A few minutes later Daniel called my mobile.

'Don't book into the hotel,' he said.

'Why?'

'We want you to stay in the flat.'

'Are you sure? What about George?'

'He wants you to stay in the flat too. Now that he's met you he thinks you're really nice, so you're staying.'

I was delighted. I stayed for two nights. Although we enjoyed ourselves it was difficult seeing them together. I knew I shouldn't really have gone but I desperately wanted to spend time with Daniel. And if that meant following him around for a couple of days with his new boyfriend, then so be it. They came to London a couple of times and I went out with them but I felt depressed afterwards, so I decided that maybe it was better to keep the friendship going by phone.

Over the next few months everything stayed the same. I finished at the LCD for good and just worked at Bolebec House. Sometimes my self-confidence was at rock bottom. I had panic attacks at things as simple as a resident's car pulling up outside. I just didn't want to talk to anyone. When they came into reception I pretended to be on the phone, so they just said hello and kept walking.

I drank in varying amounts and my depression came and went. If I saw Daniel at a club it usually ruined the night. We spoke, but it still hurt to see him. One warm Saturday night I walked up Charing Cross Road heading for GAY. Every week a different singer or group came on stage shortly after one o'clock and sang for the best part of an hour. Holly Johnson was good. Gary Newman sounded good but looked awful. Kylie Minogue had an irritating voice but drew a huge crowd; I could never understand why she was so popular on the gay scene. Joycelan Brown had a great voice. Seán Maguire was cute and Boyzone were popular. Tonight it was Boy George and I was looking forward to it. As I got nearer the club I spotted a blue Mercedes in the traffic. Damn. Daniel and his friends were going as well. I spoke to him through the open sun roof.

'All right, Daniel?'

'Hi, Andrew, I thought you'd be here tonight with Boy George being on. Do you want a lift the rest of the way?'

'No thanks. I'm almost there. Besides I bought my ticket early in the week so I don't have to queue. I'll see you in there.'

George wasn't in the car and I ignored his other friends, remembering their lies after Daniel had left me. GAY is a huge club and it's not easy to find someone unless you've already told them where you're going to be. I had a few drinks and chatted to Dennis. I hoped I wouldn't see Daniel. I really wanted to try to stay happy.

After a couple of hours Boy George came on stage and sang songs from his new album. I was standing at the very front of the stage. Behind me I could see on to the upper balcony where hundreds of people were dancing along. I spotted Dennis and a few others. Daniel was with them. I couldn't stop looking back at him and felt myself getting more and more sad. I knew Daniel and Dennis knew each other, through me, but Dennis was aware of how I felt about Daniel and I was disappointed to see him dancing with him. When Boy George left the stage I went up to see them. I stayed about five minutes and then left the club.

Tears streamed down my face as I walked back to Pimlico. I realized that as long as I stayed in London I would never get over Daniel. Every time I saw him it hurt. Everything I did reminded me of him. If I bought fresh flowers I put them into his vase. If I went out to buy a sandwich at lunch-time it reminded me of the times we stayed in watching the news and *Neighbours*. Every time I saw a blue Mercedes or a black Renault my heart missed a beat. I knew a lot of the sadness was there before I ever met him but I couldn't handle any more. If I stayed any longer I would go back to the horror of those twelve days when dying seemed like my only option. I decided go back to Dublin.

Once the decision was made I gave Magnus four weeks' notice. I was leaving London at the end of July '95. It was heart-breaking leaving the flat and memories of so many good times there with Daniel. I phoned him and told him. He wasn't upset. When I was going he would be in Penang on holiday but he promised that we'd go out for a night before he went away. On the Monday of the week before his holiday I bumped into him and George in the Edge, a gay bar in Soho Square.

'Hi, Andrew, sorry I didn't get back to you, I was really busy. Anyway, what night do you want to meet up?'

'Well, you're going to Penang on Saturday and I'm working Wednesday, Thursday and Friday so that only leaves tomorrow.'

The three of us met up in the same place the following night. We had two drinks and then went back to my flat as it was a hot night and the Edge was packed. I was so upset and sick at the way everything had gone that I hadn't eaten a single thing in three days and was beginning to feel weak. My flat stayed cool on summer nights and we sat chatting until well into the early hours. I dreaded the thought of them leaving. Would I ever see Daniel again? When it was time to go Daniel asked if I would be in the flat on Friday night after work. I said I would – my big farewell night out was planned for Saturday.

'I'll call around and see you on Friday shortly after midnight for a final drink.'

'So this isn't goodbye then?' I said, glad that I would see him one more time.

Friday night came. Daniel didn't. Nor did he phone. I sat on my bed listening to music and drinking until four in the morning. I wasn't surprised; if anything, I had been expecting it. Despite what I'd thought there would have been nothing nice about it – the two of us sitting there saying goodbye. Even now I can't find the words to describe how sad that makes me feel. On 31 July 1995 I came home.

## 15. A Time to Speak

Within months of my arrival back in Dublin my story was front-page news. Since receiving the compensation I'd always wanted to tell my story – to let people know what it was like to live with child abuse. Publisher after publisher had turned down my suggestions, so in August 1994, after yet another rejection, I had co-operated with Ciaran Byrne at the *Sunday Times* on an article about the case. Initially I gave him very general details about the story. No one was identified: I still didn't feel ready to go public and I had no intention of naming Father Payne unless I could prove he had abused others. The article said compensation of twenty-seven thousand five hundred pounds had been paid to a victim of clerical child abuse and the priest was still serving in a Dublin parish.

I was eager to see the Church's reaction. When it came, it was breathtaking.

A spokesperson from the Catholic Press Office denied any knowledge of a secret pay-off to the sexual assault victim of a Dublin-based priest.

'That is not the way the procedure works. If a priest has violated a code he is charged before a court. The issue of money does not arise.'

*Twelve months after I had been compensated?*

Bishop Thomas Flynn said, 'Any procedures followed in such cases are never viewed by the Church authorities as a substitute for civil or criminal investigation or for State guidelines.'

How could this be true when they hadn't reported Father Payne to the authorities way back in 1981?

I was amazed that an ordinary person like me was in a position to show up the Church's spokesmen and its bishops. I felt a sort of smugness about it. I knew that someday, somehow, I would prove them to be liars.

I was worried too. How could I now believe that Father Payne was not molesting boys out in Sutton? The Church had said it would look after him but it had just proven itself to be dishonest.

In April 1995, while I was still in London, I phoned Colm Keena at the *Irish Press*. I had kept his number from the time I had telephoned reporters when Father Payne's solicitors were dragging their heels over my compensation. He sent the London editor around to my flat. He looked at my documents and correspondence and verified the story for Colm Keena who then interviewed me over the phone. It was going to be a more detailed account than the *Sunday Times* article but again, neither Father Payne nor I was to be identified.

The Church was running scared. On Wednesday officials asked the *Irish Press* to hold off, promising an interview for the following day. But on Thursday they wouldn't make themselves available even by phone. Colm Keena resorted to faxing them six questions about the case. The Church refused to answer the questions and issued the following statement:

The Dublin Archdiocese is very much aware of the suffering and hurt which the abuse of a child by a priest may cause and is profoundly sorry when suffering occurs in this way. If a priest enters into a settlement with a person who has suffered abuse this is private and not a matter for public comment by the Archdiocese.

The Church refused to confirm that Father Payne was still working in a parish and would not discuss the extent of his parochial duties. I was outraged that the Church did not think it had a responsibility to address the question of whether a priest with a record of child abuse was still doing parish work. I couldn't help thinking that, messed up as I was back when I visited Bishop O'Mahony, my gut instinct was right: I had come away very uneasy about his view that he had heard no complaints against Father Payne and therefore Father Payne could not be abusing anyone else. The way the Church was handling the issue now showed that my unease then was more than justified.

When the interview was published, a spokesman for the Catholic Press Office was asked to explain its August 1994 statement that the issue of money did not arise in dealing with cases of priests molesting children since it was now clear that the opposite was the case.

'I responded that such payments are not made by the Church,' the spokesman said, explaining a response which had been misleading at best. 'On that basis they [the diocesan authorities] denied this specific instance, but they [reporters] had not put that specific instance to us. You are making an assumption that the Church made or approved of any payments and that is only an assumption.' The dishonesty behind these words would soon be revealed.

Now I had to make a phone call I had been dreading. For the first time I had to speak to my parents about what was going on. Of course they were both very upset but they were totally supportive. I was glad I was in London and they were in Dublin so they could have time to get used to my situation and I could get used to them knowing. But we didn't have long to adjust: within days of speaking to them I had a call from *The Gay Byrne Show* asking me to fly to Dublin that

weekend to record an interview with Joe Duffy for trans-
mission on Monday morning.

My father asked if I was sure I wanted to do it: people might
recognize my voice. I wasn't sure I was prepared for what
might happen afterwards, but I was determined to do it anyway. I wasn't ready to use my own name but I was very
tempted to identify Father Payne. I thought of all that I had
been through and all that I had lost. Things that should be
good were contaminated. Like the birth of my niece. Audrey
and Pat had Laura in June 1994. I came home to see her and
they asked me to be her godfather. People teased me, telling
me it wasn't all glamour – turning up with big presents on big
occasions – but that one of my new responsibilities would be
changing her nappies. I should have been able to laugh –
knowing how fanatical I was about cleanliness it was a big
joke – and I should have been happy to be part of her life.
Instead, the jokes put me on edge. I did not want to change
her nappies because I was so afraid anyone might ever think
that because I had been abused I might do something similar
and I didn't want to leave myself open to any allegations. In
short, I was paranoid.

It was the same over the next couple of years. I wouldn't
take Laura to the shops on my own if I was feeling down or
self-conscious. I was afraid of what people meeting us in
the street might think. I was so angry: I was quite sure I only
had these feelings because of my experiences with Father
Payne. Nearly twenty years later something which should
have been fun – my relationship with my baby niece – was
being affected.

That's why I wanted to speak out. To show the hypocrisy
of the Church saying that it was very much aware of the
'suffering and hurt' caused by its abusing priests and its dishonesty in pretending that I didn't exist. Now I knew it was

rotten to the core. It's one thing to be at home reading stories in the papers or watching the news and wondering just who is telling the truth. But when it's your own story you can see all the lies and you just want to go out and tell everyone.

I knew some people might recognize my voice on the radio but I didn't care; what was happening was more important. I knew that if I named Father Payne reporters would be on his doorstep in minutes and then the Church would have to start answering questions. But I decided to bite my tongue and hold back: I still didn't know whether he'd gone on to abuse anyone else and it wouldn't have been fair to name him out of anger at the hierarchy's arrogance and indifference.

After the interview I expected the media to put pressure on the Church to start explaining its actions and to speak about its policy of moving paedophile priests from parish to parish. But that didn't happen. Reaction was muted, possibly because no one was identified. But I got many telephone calls from other people who had been abused. They just wanted to talk to someone they knew would understand because we'd all had similar experiences.

I felt sure the story had not yet run its course. The media would start investigating and others who had been abused were bound to note that they were as entitled to compensation as I was. I hoped some of them would take action.

In July the *Sunday Times* asked me to write an article to go alongside a news item on the subject. I agreed and I said I would no longer hide behind anonymity. I didn't think it was right to carry on hiding when so much of the story was already public. It sent out a message that I thought I had something to be ashamed of, that somehow there was a stigma attached to having been abused. Maybe there had been in the past but it was not right to carry on as though I accepted this stigma. If I spoke out, others might find it easier to do the same. The paper took photographs and I put my name to the article. So did the *Sunday World* and the *Sunday Express*.

Chris Moore, who had made a programme detailing the activities of Father Brendan Smyth, the priest whose story woke people up to the nature and extent of clerical sex abuse and to the Church's negligent handling of the issue, contacted me in September asking me to do an interview for his follow-up programme for UTV. I agreed, and the interview was due to be shown in late October.

Bishop O'Mahony had written to me three times since December 1994 asking how I was and inviting me to get in touch. When I returned to Dublin in July 1995 I decided to take him up on his offer. I wanted to know more about the extent of child abuse within the Church and its handling of the issue. I went to his house for a second time.

Bishop O'Mahony said he would not answer questions about Father Payne, nor would he deal with the Church's policy on paedophile priests. He advised me to address those questions to someone else. He was delighted to be able to tell me, after all these years, that my rejection from the priesthood had nothing to do with my allegations against Father Payne. However, he did not know why I had been turned down. I told him about how bad things had been in recent years. It was important to me that someone in the hierarchy should be given a first-hand account of the lasting effects of child abuse. When they spoke about suffering and hurt they should know what they were talking about.

In the *Sunday World* I read a story by Seán Boyne that two people, who said they knew me from Cabra, were alleging that they had also been abused by Father Payne. I asked him to give them my number but I got no calls. I wondered about people I knew at that time – Simon, Kevin and others. Could they really have been abused by Father Payne? Putting two and two together from what Seán Boyne said to me I was sure they were the people who had spoken to him, but obviously he couldn't reveal their identities. I took a chance and phoned Kevin. He was out. The following day I bumped into him around Cabra.

'Hi, Kevin, how are you? Long time no see.'

'Ah, Andrew, how's it going? How's everything?'

We got through the small talk.

'I believe you phoned the house looking for me,' he said.

'I did, yeah. I don't know if you saw it, but there was an article about me in the *Sunday World* in July.'

'I saw it, yeah.'

'The following week there was another article which said two other people from around Cabra claimed the same thing had happened to them and – I hope you don't mind me asking – I was wondering if you were one of those people?'

'I was, yeah,' said Kevin.

Kevin said another friend of his, Edward (not his real name), was the other person referred to in the article. I knew Edward just to say hello to.

Now I knew for sure that I hadn't been the only one and that Father Payne had abused others. But knowing that just raised lots more questions. First, how effective could Father Payne's treatment have been? Part of the treatment of paedophiles involves admission of guilt. If he had admitted abusing Kevin and Edward and not just me, when he was first challenged back in 1981, then surely the Church would have made some effort to contact them discreetly to see if they were all right or if they needed any help. They would, after all, have been around the same age as me at the time, fifteen or sixteen. But that did not happen. So was it the case that Father Payne only partially admitted his guilt? And therefore could his treatment have been in any way effective? And did that not increase the likelihood that he would have gone on to abuse others in his new parish? Given that Kevin, Edward and myself had all been abused at around the same time I still didn't know if Father Payne had molested anyone else after he had been moved.

But at the end of September the decision to name Father Payne or not was taken out of my hands. Ursula Halligan had asked me for an interview for RTÉ's current affairs programme, *Prime Time*. I was keen to do it but had promised Chris Moore that I wouldn't give any interviews until after his programme was screened. I watched the *Prime Time* programme, flabbergasted, as Ursula Halligan revealed that Father Ivan Payne, associate presiding judge of the Archdiocese of Dublin's Marriage Tribunal, was the subject of a Garda investigation as a result of allegations that he had abused children. I was shocked and pleased. If the allegations were true, and I believed they were, then he deserved to be named.

The programme also challenged Archbishop Connell's May interview in which he had said, 'I have compensated no one. Diocesan funds have not been used in any way for the purpose of compensation.' It revealed that the Archbishop had loaned Father Payne the money to make the settlement out of those very same diocesan funds which had not been used *in any way* for the purposes of compensation. And the Catholic Press Office telling the *Irish Press* that reporters' assertions that the Church had approved the payment of compensation were 'only an assumption' – that was blown out of the water too.

The old adage that once yōu start with a lie many more will follow seemed to have taken on a life of its own. Although he had been told of my allegations in 1981, and had acknowledged my April 1993 letter to the Archbishop by telephone and in writing, this did not stop Monsignor Alex Stenson telling parishioners in Sutton that he knew nothing about

Father Payne's alleged activities, that he had worked with Father Payne for years and was as shocked by the allegations as they were.

I had taken up Bishop O'Mahony's suggestion that I address my questions on the Church's policy on clerical child abuse to someone else and had sent a letter to Cardinal Daly (see Appendix).

I asked him what treatment paedophile priests received after admitting their offences, how effective it was and how that was assessed, how the Church authorities knew if it was safe to put a priest with a record of child abuse back into the community, how many priests were facing allegations of abusing children, and how many of them were serving priests. I asked him to explain a word Archbishop Connell had used in a letter to my mother when he said priests with a record of child abuse were 'monitored'.

The reply (see Appendix) came five weeks later. Cardinal Daly said his concern was that the offender received the most effective treatment, 'not only for his own benefit but to protect others in the future'. He said that in deciding whether to re-admit a priest who had offended to active ministry, a bishop was guided by the clinical advice he received, which would include advice on aftercare, review and appropriate supervision. A bishop, he said, would also have 'careful regard to pastoral considerations attendant on any particular appointment' and would 'wholeheartedly participate in this process where appropriate'. On the subject of numbers the Cardinal said he was concerned about the allegations against a number of priests. Many of these allegations were of wrongdoing a considerable time previously and each had its own particular circumstances. He was not aware of the number of allegations recently or in the past.

Talk of clinical aftercare, appropriate supervision and

review, and pastoral considerations attendant on any particular appointment did not leave me any the wiser. Who was supervising Father Payne as he went about his pastoral duties in Sutton? The people closest to him would have been the other priests in the parish – did that mean they knew of his past and were monitoring him in some way? When asked this question later, at a parish meeting in Sutton, they wouldn't answer – for 'legal reasons', they said.

What was said about taking care of pastoral considerations – particularly not putting other children at risk – didn't add up either. The Catholic Press Office had declared that although Father Payne had been a priest at two north Dublin parishes, his job as canon lawyer with the Marriage Tribunal meant he had worked at Archbishop's House virtually all of the time. That wasn't how I remembered it. Father Payne had been involved with the altar boys, the folk group and the youth club, Our Lady's Hospital for Sick Children and the Sunshine House for Poor Children.

An elderly parishioner in Sutton told the *Irish Independent*, 'I can't believe he did this, he was the best of priests. He married, christened and buried people and even since he left he's been invited back to do weddings because he was so well liked.'

A sixteen-year-old girl said vague rumours about the priest had been circulating since the previous year: 'But I don't think anyone believed them and I still find it hard to believe now. He was one of the nicest priests I've met and he was really easy to talk to in confession.'

Another teenager, a boy of eighteen, talked about how active Father Payne was in the community. 'He was very involved in the youth club and other groups so most people would have known him and he was very popular with everyone.'

So why was the Catholic Press Office telling the media he was spending 'virtually all of his time' at Archbishop's House? It seemed that the 'careful regard to pastoral considerations attendant on any particular appointment' was just lip service.

I received sympathetic letters from Cardinal Daly and Bishop O'Mahony which, given that I had received a payment for admitted abuse by Father Payne, led me to believe that they accepted the facts of my case.

'Thank you so much for your kind letter of 25 January. I was very sorry to hear that you had been through such a difficult and painful time since we last met,' wrote Bishop O'Mahony on 2 April 1995. 'If you would wish, I would be very happy to see you on your next visit to Dublin.'

'I am sorry for your distress and I offer you my sympathy,' said Cardinal Daly on 18 August. 'I wish to emphasize again my concern for you,' he wrote a month later. 'I am aware of the great hurt and distress which you still feel.'

With such senior Churchmen in the know, and with a settlement made, why was the Catholic Press Office fobbing off reporters with vague and dishonest statements? Why was Sutton curate Father Ciaran O'Carroll telling his congregation, 'Everyone is innocent until proven guilty', as he did the Sunday after the *Prime Time* programme? He told them that he had been concerned about the source of the money for any compensation paid and had gone to Monsignor John Wilson of the Archbishop's Financial Secretariat to find out if any of it had come from Sutton. 'The answer is no,' he told his congregation. 'He says he got it from an administration fund. I don't know where an administration fund comes from but I know this, it did not come from Sutton.'

The local money was safe. What about the local children?

In January 1996 an advisory committee set up by the bishops to lay down guidelines on dealing with clerical sex abuse finally reported. The sixty-seven-page document, 'Child Sexual Abuse: Framework for a Church Response', was two years in the making and was put together by six lay people and seven religious including Jim Cantwell, Director of the Catholic Press and Information Office, and the one and only Monsignor Alex Stenson, Professor of Canon Law.

I welcomed the report but felt it was flawed. It was good that the Church detailed the effects of abuse – even if this was in just three paragraphs. Never again could bishops say that they did not understand the gravity of child abuse.

It went on to recommend a number of appointments in each of the twenty-six dioceses: a delegate to oversee the handling of cases; a support person to liaise with people making complaints and help them through the process, an advisor to liaise with accused priests or religious while they were being investigated, and a panel of experts – including a childcare specialist and canon and civil lawyers – to advise the diocese when relevant.

Something which attracted a lot of media attention was the document's guideline on reporting allegations: 'In all instances where it is known or suspected that a child has been, or is being, sexually abused by a priest or religious the matter would be reported to the civil authorities.' This was widely taken to mean that all cases would be reported to the police or the health boards. But that's not what it says. Rather than saying all *allegations* of child abuse would be reported, it only recommends the reporting of cases where abuse is 'known or suspected' – a crucial difference. In other words, a diocese's delegate, support person and advisor would establish for themselves whether an allegation had the essence of truth about it before reporting it to the authorities. This was totally unacceptable. Given its record, the Church could not be trusted to deal with such issues internally.

Whatever its shortcomings, the guidelines document was a start. After six months I decided to establish the extent to which they had been implemented. I wrote to the bishop or archbishop in each diocese asking questions based on the report's recommendations. I asked the name of his delegate, support person and advisor and what their training was. I asked who was on the advisory panel. I asked what was being done to raise awareness of the issue amongst the clergy. I asked each bishop if he could guarantee that all allegations of child abuse by priests or religious would be reported to the authorities. And I asked how many priests had been moved between parishes as a result of allegations between the time of the bishop's appointment and the publication of the guidelines.

I asked a lot of questions. I got very few answers.

Bishop Brendan Comiskey's secretary was the first to reply, with a brief acknowledgement and nothing else.

The Bishop of Cork and Ross, Michael Murphy, wrote that any complaints in his diocese had always been dealt with appropriately, and he did not answer my questions (see Appendix).

From Kildare and Leighlin Bishop Laurence Ryan said 'the information you request is being sent to you'. It never arrived.

Finally, Archbishop Connell's secretary said that the Archbishop was implementing the guidelines in full – but he too did not answer my questions (see Appendix).

Then I had a long letter from Jim Cantwell (see Appendix). He said the bishops had been in touch with him regarding my letter and he was responding for them. Despite its length the letter told me very little. He said the name of each diocese's delegate had been 'made public' – which made the bishops' reticence seem odd – but to protect their privacy the names of the support person, advisor and members of the advisory panel were not generally being publicized. He didn't include a list of delegates' names. He said that between them all the dioceses had held information days for their priests and religious and every priest in the country had received a copy of the framework document.

On reporting, he quoted the words of the advisory committee: 'In making its recommendations in regard to reporting, the advisory committee considers to be paramount the safety and protection of children and the need to prevent, where possible, further abuse.' He concluded that he was not in a position to provide figures for the number of priests against whom allegations had been made who had been moved on to other parishes.

Jim Cantwell had responded to my questions. He had even answered some of them and, as a bonus, he had given me a lot of information I hadn't asked for. But how could the director of the Catholic Press Office be in a position to know the extent to which the guidelines had been introduced in every diocese in the country, when the bishops were not answerable to him in any way? Why couldn't the bishops reply for themselves?

My questions were very specific yet Jim Cantwell's reply was very general. Not one bishop gave me the name of the person he had appointed as the diocesan delegate, despite the framework document saying that the delegate 'should be widely identified and known as such to facilitate easy access by all'.

I had asked for a guarantee that all allegations of child abuse would be reported to the civil authorities. Not one bishop would give it.

Finally, if Jim Cantwell knew so much about every diocese in the country, why couldn't he answer my question about the numbers of paedophile priests moved between parishes? The old practice – which amounted to a policy – was to move abusing priests to new parishes, sometimes after 'treatment', sometimes not. In an interview with Australian television Bishop Thomas Flynn said he was so naïve that he thought all a paedophile needed was confession.

*Confession?*

Three 'Hail Marys' and they'd never do it again?

How many times had this happened? How many priests with a record of child abuse were in parishes with access to children?

'I am not in a position to provide the information you request,' was all Jim Cantwell would say. Cardinal Daly had told me that in all cases where a priest was moved on to a new parish, the decision to allow him to continue as a priest was based, amongst other things, on appropriate supervision. But how could the Church supervise its paedophile priests if it didn't know how many there were?

# 16. Facing Father Payne

Returning to Dublin in July 1995, I had no idea what life had in store for me. The uncertainty was terrifying. My sister put me up in the spare room of her house in Cabra. I stopped drinking for a second time but this lasted only three months. I got a part-time job at the *Big Issue* helping the vendors in the city centre. I had no idea what I wanted to do. Friends encouraged me to take some night courses to see if I could find anything I liked. In September I started in a computer applications class. I wasn't attempting to rebuild my life – I wasn't that ambitious – I just wanted to be seen to be doing something. After passing the exams in 1996 I moved on to diploma level and I realized that I was picking things up quicker than the others in the classroom and I liked what I was doing. No one seemed to notice that I sometimes turned up drunk.

Compared to London, Dublin's gay scene was small. I went to the George on South Great George's Street a few times and drank myself into oblivion. I only went off with a guy if he had a place. I met Val, Stephen and a few others from the Navan Road for the occasional 'few scoops', though I had more than a few. My drinking had me in a mess: generally I was afraid and paranoid and knew I needed to try giving it up again.

I had my last drink on Sunday, 23 March 1997. I had known for some time that if I was ever to accept and like myself as the person I really was, then drowning in scotch was not the answer. For years alcohol gave me confidence and made me feel better about myself. But it wasn't working any more: now I felt guilty every time I drank and finally I understood what my doctor had tried to get into my head years previously: alcohol made everything – anxiety, depression, paranoia – worse. I couldn't hold drink the way I used to. Now I got drunk easily and shocked myself at the state I sometimes got into on nights out with friends.

But even knowing all this, giving up drink was a painful wrench. Not only was there the fear that I had tried living sober before and it hadn't worked and I'd been miserable, but also I knew I was at the end of my life's drinking. This was it. The end. For ever. And I had no idea how I was going to not drink.

On that Sunday morning I was up at about half past eleven, my stomach in knots as I tried to brush my teeth, something I was used to after years of drinking. Having finished off the scotch the night before, I started drinking vodka to try to calm my stomach and I needed at least two large ones before I felt relaxed. I drank all day and picked at an evening meal. At six feet tall I weighed just nine and a half stone. I'd always hated being so skinny yet I'd preferred to drink rather than eat. I dragged myself to yet another programme meeting and listened for even a word that would help me not to buy a bottle of scotch the following day. I went home and poured myself one last drink. It took nearly two hours to finish it. I was truly beaten. For the first time in my life I really didn't want to drink any more, yet I knew I would need a huge amount of help to stop.

I went to my GP the following morning and he put me on another course of Librium. For the rest of that week I spent nearly every waking moment in the company of people from the programme. Alcoholics. Alcoholics, just like me.

Recovering from the physical and emotional damage I'd

done to myself by drinking had to start before I could really look at any other issues – like taking on the Church and Father Payne again. I had to learn to like, accept and feel comfortable with myself sober instead of thinking of myself as the person I became when drinking.

It was good to be at home and have the support of family and friends. They hadn't seen all of my drinking career, but they'd seen some of the worst of it over these past few months and they were not just pleased, but relieved, that I had finally faced up to my problem.

With so much publicity about the criminal investigation into Father Payne now they were in the picture about that part of my life too, which was a great help and source of strength, though being a sort of public figure in the streets where I had grown up was a bit weird and funny. It was so ironic: as a child I had dreamed of being a priest and getting people's admiration, but I had made my mark by bringing to light the dark side of the life I had so desired and challenging the institution I had so admired. As I popped round to the shops on the Cabra Road there were plenty of funny looks and the occasional comment. I was amazed at the number of people who seemed to think I was deaf. *Oh look, that's yer man, isn't it?* At worst people pretended not to see me, but most were kind.

After thirteen years I saw Father Payne again on 17 October 1997 at his first appearance at the Dublin Circuit Criminal Court. Because of the settlement in my case, it was being tried separately. Another case, based on a sample group of complaints from eight other young men, was to be tried after mine. I brought a friend with me because I knew I'd be nervous, but I didn't expect to feel as bad as I did. I stood at the back of Court 24, a small room, and observed

Father Payne as he sat no more than four feet away from me. His neat and prematurely white hair was tossed; he wore dark trousers and a dark shirt over which he had a pale green mac tied with a knotted belt. His face looked troubled and tired. He looked nervous. Occasionally he leaned forward and buried his head in his hands. He had the appearance of a broken man.

I felt sick and guilty. Had I reduced him to this?

In a way I had. If I'd kept my mouth shut he would still be sitting on the Marriage Tribunal and working in Sutton. Instead he was sitting on a court bench, flanked by dubious-looking characters whose company he wouldn't have liked at all. Of course he'd brought this on himself, but that didn't change how I felt.

As the cases were called out the defendants had to go to the front of the court and stand in front of Judge Cyril Kelly. I didn't think Father Payne would have to do the same thing as the other defendants. I assumed he would be treated differently. But there's no special treatment for priests any more and eventually he took his place before the judge. The crowded courtroom was noisy and I couldn't hear what happened during his brief appearance. As soon as I saw him prepare to leave I hurried to the reception area because otherwise he'd walk right past me on his way out of the courtroom and I didn't want that.

Afterwards, my solicitor and the detective in charge of the investigation explained that Father Payne had pleaded not guilty to the charges of assault against me and a three-day trial was scheduled for January. I was amazed that he had stood there and lied. It reminded me that there were two Father Paynes: the one that preached honesty and the one that had lied in front of everyone in court. I thought about my own feelings of guilt and wondered if he too felt at all guilty for putting me, or even threatening to put me, through a trial. Did it not occur to him that he had put me through enough already? Did he think of me at all?

Through the next three months the trial was like a dark cloud hanging over me. I hardly slept the night before it was due to start. On Monday, 26 January we all returned to the court. Father Payne arrived looking much smarter than he had in October – more like the smartly dressed Father Payne I remembered. Then word came that there was unlikely to be a trial after all – Father Payne was pleading guilty. The case was far down the day's schedule but because of the seniority of Father Payne's counsel, Michael McDowell SC, Judge Cyril Kelly called the case early.

Father Payne again took his place in the dock. The court-room was quiet as the charges were read out. Detective Sergeant Bernard – known as Brian – Sherry urged me to make sure I listened carefully so I would hear Father Payne's guilty plea. He knew it was important for the victim of the crime – me in this case – to hear the offender – Father Payne – finally admit his guilt. When he pleaded guilty I could hardly hear him. But I heard enough. Mr McDowell said his client would be taking a certain course of action in relation to allegations from eight other boys on the following Friday. This was legal-speak for saying he would plead guilty to all the other allegations against him.

This time I didn't run and hide when I saw Father Payne prepare to leave. I stood right beside Brian Sherry. As he passed us he kept his eyes on the detective and didn't acknowledge me in any way.

On Friday it was back to Court 24 again. It was packed but when Father Payne entered the dock the place went silent. Thirteen sample charges were read out and he pleaded guilty to each one. It seemed to go on for ever. The dates of the assaults ran from 1967 to 1987 – some of them long after the Church had been told about my allegations back in 1981. Some of the offences were committed in Our Lady's Hospital for Sick Children in Crumlin, others in Drimnagh, Glasnevin and Sutton. From the time Father Payne was a young curate in his early twenties he had been abusing children.

Several weeks later I went to the Dáil and handed in a letter for the attention of the Taoiseach urging him to consider setting up a full public inquiry into the way the Catholic Church had handled allegations of child abuse against its priests. I didn't think there was anything unique in the way Father Payne had been moved to Sutton after I complained. And I didn't think it was unusual that having been moved he went on to abuse children again.

I pointed out that inquiries had been set up to look into the contamination of blood and blood products, the finances of a former Taoiseach, questionable banking services sold by National Irish Bank, and allegations of corruption in the beef industry and in the planning process. The Irish Amateur Swimming Association was investigated following abuse allegations against just two coaches. Surely it was appropriate that the widespread sexual abuse of children by Catholic priests and consistent cover-up by the hierarchy should also be investigated independently to establish what had gone wrong in the past and to ensure that such abuse could never so easily be repeated.

I added that the State had a responsibility to investigate because it had given control of education and childcare to the Church. That put priests and religious in positions of trust where those who were inclined had easy access to potential victims of their abusive behaviour.

On Monday, 27 April we were all back in Court 24 for what turned out to be a two-day sentence hearing. It was still incredibly hard to imagine Father Payne going to prison. On some level I was – and am – concerned for him as a human being, as someone who was a big part of my past. In 1981 I worried about how he would feel when he heard that I had told on him, and in 1992 I wondered about the impact of my first solicitor's letter. I just had to give myself permission to feel concern for him – I suppose this was good in that it told me I hadn't been eaten up by bitterness – whilst at the same time knowing and believing that in speaking out I had done the right thing.

Detective Sherry outlined the nine cases against Father Payne. I was the only victim who wanted to make a statement about the effects the abuse had had on me. I had been assured by both the prosecution and Brian Sherry that I could read from my prepared statement, but when I sat in the witness box, only feet away from Father Payne, Judge Kelly said I could only read it if both the prosecution and the defence had seen it first. I had to put the statement away and answer questions about the effects on my life – first from counsel for the prosecution. I was nervous and not prepared for questions and didn't feel I really got my life's experiences across properly. Mr McDowell then rose and said my evidence was fully accepted by Father Payne and would not be challenged. But I still didn't feel it had gone well.

People spoke for Father Payne. His sister, Jacinta Loftus, had flown in from Virginia, USA to give her evidence. She said their mother, a midwife, had been a very dominant person while their father, a detective, was more gentle and easy-going. She said that as a boy her brother Ivan had been shy, introverted and quite a loner. He was the only boy in the family and was put on a pedestal by his mother.

Also speaking for Father Payne was consultant psychiatrist Dr Patrick Walsh, director of the Granada Institute which treats paedophiles. He told the court that Father Payne's offending behaviour was 'regressive' rather than 'compulsive-fixated' – not terms I understood, but according to him it meant that Father Payne's form of paedophilia was more receptive to treatment than other kinds. Dr Walsh was very keen that Father Payne's time in prison be kept as short as possible so he could continue treatment he had already commenced. On day two, Dr Walsh's Granada Institute colleague, Marie Keenan, a consultant psychotherapist, said Father Payne's continued treatment was very important and she was sure that the places provided for such treatment in prison were totally inadequate since there were almost 250 sex offenders in prison, with only ten treatment places available.

Mr McDowell spoke for his client at great length. Apart from talking about the nature of Father Payne's tendencies, he said Father Payne was not to blame for the Church's mistakes in managing him after my initial allegations in 1981. And it wasn't his fault if I was disappointed at not being accepted into the priesthood.

As I sat at the back of the courtroom with other people Father Payne had abused, I was startled when Mr McDowell said he had one more witness to call. And Father Payne himself, distinguished-looking as always, took his place on the stand. I tried to look up but realized that it would be hard to avoid making eye contact with him, so all I could do was look at the ground as he spoke. Up until now I had stolen the occasional glance at him as he sat alone in the corner of the room. It made me feel so sad to hear the man I had once held in such high regard sound so broken. And broken he was. Although he didn't actually break down he came close to it and his voice was shaky and emotional. Listening to him speak, my feelings of guilt came flooding back. If I had said nothing he might not be in this awful position.

He said he wanted to acknowledge that he had hurt many people by his behaviour, including his victims, their families and friends as well as his own family and friends. 'I am sorry for the hurt I have caused them all. I want them to know I deeply regret the hurt I have caused them.'

I was at a loss to know what to make of his apology. He certainly had the appearance of a man full of remorse, but when I first got to know him I had learned that there was more to this man than his appearance. As I listened to him speak in court, I had no way of knowing whether this was the nice, amiable Father Payne sincerely sorry for his actions, or the manipulative abuser using all those around him, including us again, to benefit his own situation, wanting to sound convincing for the judge. It's not that I could say he was being insincere, but part of his legacy is that I have no way of knowing when to believe him.

At the end of day two Judge Kelly said he had heard so much evidence he was not prepared to announce the sentence straight away and would take some time to consider the matter: 23 June was set as the sentence day. He told Father Payne that he would now be taken into custody to start serving whatever sentence would be announced in June. I left the courtroom immediately. Everyone seemed disappointed that a conclusion had not been reached. I spoke briefly to the press and got away quickly. I knew Father Payne would be leaving in handcuffs and it was not a sight I wanted to see. Nor did I want to make that experience any more difficult for him by standing there, seeming to gloat.

Later that evening I saw the scene on the six o'clock news. It was awful. But I reminded myself that Father Payne was getting what he deserved for what he had done.

On 9 June 1998 the Taoiseach, Bertie Ahern, turned down my request for a public inquiry (see Appendix), saying that the Church was not a public body and inquiries could only be established 'for the purpose of inquiring into definite matters of urgent public importance'. I thought there was hardly an issue of more urgent public importance than child abuse.

He said such a tribunal would be legally challengeable on the grounds that it would be unfair to single out and focus on the Church. But was it unfair to single out the IASA, a sporting organization, when people in other types of organization abused children? It didn't make much sense to me. Nearly fifty priests and religious had been convicted of child sexual abuse, whilst just two swimming coaches had allegations made against them. One hundred recommendations were made for changes to the functioning of the IASA but the Church didn't warrant an investigation. It sounded to me like Mr Ahern was reluctant to challenge a powerful institution which still has a number of devoted members – and voters. Perhaps he would think again if those abused in schools, hospitals or in care decided to sue the State as well as the Church.

On Tuesday, 23 June 1998 Judge Kelly sentenced Father Payne to eight terms of six years, two of five years and three of four years – all to run concurrently. The last four years were suspended on the understanding that he continue treatment on his release. This meant he was looking at two years behind bars. I considered he was a very lucky man to be getting away with a two-year sentence for two decades of child sexual abuse, but I had prepared myself to try to accept whatever sentence was handed down. We had presented our cases and the judicial system had to take its course.

The Director of Public Prosecutions saw things differently

and appealed the leniency of the sentence to the Court of Criminal Appeal. The court reinstated the last four years of Father Payne's sentence so now he was to serve the full six years.

## 17. Life After Abuse

In early October 2002 a reporter phoned to say Father Payne was being released from prison later that month. I thought sex offenders did not qualify for early release and had to serve their full sentences, so I hadn't expected his release until April 2004. After several phone calls to the prison service I was put through to a victim liaison officer who confirmed that Father Payne was to be released on 26 October: like all prisoners, he was entitled to remission of one quarter of his sentence if he was of good behaviour during his time in custody.

The liaison officer said that if I had wanted to be informed of Father Payne's release date I should have told him – which was a bit of a Catch 22 since I only found out he existed when Father Payne was about to be released.

Within a short time the phone was ringing off the hook and it was clear that Father Payne's release from prison was going to generate a lot of publicity. Once I had accepted that he was to come out of prison early I considered that justice had run its course and the best use of the publicity would be to draw attention to the few treatment places for sex offenders in prisons. It was also an opportunity for people to consider the implications for communities where offenders try to make their homes. Should everyone in an area be informed? Should no one? What are parents' rights? What rights should people have if they object to having a convicted sex offender in their midst? Recent regulations are that convicted sex offenders must notify the Gardaí, who are responsible for maintaining the sex offenders' register, of their address. How useful is such a register?

Although my attempts to provoke debate were reported, they fell on deaf ears – until Father Payne was released.

Within weeks newspapers reported that he was living in a luxurious apartment in Clarion Quay near the city centre. A march was planned, apparently to run Father Payne out of the area. I was horrified and distressed. And I was also concerned for Father Payne. In interviews I made it clear that I did not support such actions. The system that allowed released sex offenders to live anywhere they wanted was not of Father Payne's making and he should not have been blamed for it. Responsibility for the system lay with the Government, so if people wanted to protest they should have gone to Bertie Ahern's home instead of Father Payne's. If they wanted something done maybe they should have sought a meeting with Father Payne's former defence counsel, the Minister for Justice, Michael McDowell.

Over the next few days callers to radio shows said it was the Church's place to care for him and make sure he was not in a position to re-offend easily. This was nonsense. It is the State's responsibility to manage the release of sex offenders from prison and to ensure that children are not put at risk from someone known to be a danger to them. The State needed to rise to its responsibility.

At every opportunity when talking to reporters I tried to express my anger at the Taoiseach's failings in dealing with the Church's negligence in the matter of child sexual abuse by its priests. I really wanted someone with influence to take up the cause. In early 2002 the BBC screened the documentary *Suing the Pope* which detailed allegations of child sexual abuse against priests in the Diocese of Ferns and raised more questions about the Catholic Church's handling of those allegations. The Taoiseach said he did not want to cross the line between politics and religion, that it was not a matter for politicians. Did he not understand that raping and assaulting children has nothing to do with religion?

His health minister, Micheál Martin, showed better judgement in asking senior counsel George Birmingham to conduct a preliminary inquiry in Ferns and report back on what type of structure would be needed to carry out a full and independent investigation into the diocese. While this was a move I applauded, I wanted an inquiry which was capable – if the need arose – of looking at every diocese in the country.

A *Prime Time* special screened on 17 October 2002 did the trick. Such was the public outrage at the forensic detailing of eight priests' abuse of children in Dublin and the subsequent reaction by the archdiocese of Dublin that momentum was gathering by the hour. If ever the time was right to launch an inquiry it was now. The Taoiseach said nothing of any substance but Michael McDowell TD seemed to be considering what form the Government's response should take. Colm O'Gorman, director of One In Four, the support organization for victims of sex abuse, invited me to accompany him to a meeting with Minister McDowell. The meeting lasted just under an hour and I came away convinced that at long last an inquiry would be set up.

We agreed that a new structure with statutory powers, rather than a cumbersome tribunal, should be set up, not only to investigate the Church's handling of allegations in Dublin, but to respond to similar issues in the future from other parts of the country. And it should consider not only the Church's actions but the response of agencies such as the Gardaí and health boards when they became aware of allegations, whether these were reported to them officially or not.

At the time of writing it is clear that such an inquiry will be launched and it is only a matter of when, not if.

As for me, I'm doing all right. Looking back, I see that I have been very hurt by all that happened. Naturally, some of the hurt stems from my parents splitting up when I was young and the loss of a normal happy-go-lucky childhood. But Father Payne – in the way of sexual predators – spotted the resulting vulnerability and exploited it. And I am sure his abuse was the major source of my feelings of anxiety, fear, trauma, worry, guilt and shame later in life. I feel I was robbed of the opportunity to grow up and develop in a normal way.

Of course I wish I had been a stronger child and that I could have stopped the abuse sooner, but the simple fact is I wasn't and I couldn't.

Am I therefore partly to blame?

No, I am not.

Unless you have been abused it may seem odd that I could not stop Father Payne for three years, but I just couldn't. True, he was never violent and never threatened me but control comes in many forms. I was an altar boy and in my little world the Church was everything. Priests were the most important, respected and powerful people I knew. I was also sexually naïve and totally innocent. All I could understand, especially in the early stages, was that what was going on was wrong and that despite myself I was in the middle of it. It took until I was almost doing my Inter before I could eventually get away.

And for most of those three years I spent a lot of time telling myself that nothing was really going on. Even on those Saturday afternoons I just concentrated on the television. I was so determined to keep the abuse from myself that there was no way I would have been capable of telling anyone else.

Being a paedophile, Father Payne would have known that.

He would have known that my silence was not based on consent but on fear and shame. He would have known that I couldn't tell anyone what he was doing. I wasn't a child he'd abducted from a playground; I was part of his world. He gave me lifts in his car. He visited my home and had tea with my mother. He had me serving him on the altar as he said Mass for my family and neighbours. He knew he was safe. That is the nature of the child abuser.

There is nothing wrong with being a quiet, shy or even weak child. The wrong is to exploit that child as Father Payne did. Stopping child abuse is not something any child should be responsible for. Although for a long time I did feel partly responsible, the blame is now back where it belongs.

I was not unique. In fact, I was typical. The majority of children being abused don't tell anyone what's happening. Even as adults most people never tell anyone, although thankfully that's beginning to change now that the issue is out in the open.

I do not blame my sexuality for the abuse, nor do I blame the abuse for my sexuality. I don't feel that I invited Father Payne's attentions by making it obvious that I was gay; it wasn't obvious to me until many years later. I was quiet, polite and friendly towards him. That was it. There was nothing about me or my behaviour that could have been taken as an invitation for sexual activity. Not from a twelve-year-old boy. Vulnerability, maybe an over-eagerness to be friendly and helpful, to get approval – that could be exploited, but it couldn't be mistaken for something else. And even if I had turned up at his house with pink hair, stilettos and a packet of condoms it wouldn't have excused him laying a finger on me.

I believe I was gay from birth even if I didn't acknowledge it for many years. There is no link between being abused and being gay. My 'straight' years were not a rejection of my homosexuality in reaction to my experiences with Father Payne. I think accepting my sexuality came late because in my teenage years, when I should have been out at discos and experimenting, I assumed that sexuality was irrelevant to me because I was going to be a priest and would never have sex anyway. Although I knew I found fellas attractive, it didn't occur to me that it meant anything or could develop into anything more. A bit like now – I still find girls attractive but I'm not into having sex with them.

Apart from what happened with Father Payne, in which I was passive, my sexual life started late. At first it felt natural to go with girls. It took some time before I knew for sure I really wanted something else. If I had started going out with girls when I was fourteen the realization that my preference lay elsewhere would, I feel, have come sooner.

So I don't think Father Payne made me gay. But I do think he caused the sexual difficulties I've had in my relationships, both gay and straight. At a time when my whole personality, my emotional, intellectual and sexual self, was developing, he made me think that sexual activity and sexual abuse are one and the same thing. As an adult it has been very difficult to undo that.

Of course, I know physical intimacy and abuse are not the same – not remotely so. I know if I go to a club and then spend the night with someone I've met that I'm not abusing him, though we are using each other. It's easy to use someone I have no feelings for, especially if he is using me in the same way at the same time.

But what's logical and what's instinctive can be two different things: feelings come out of a primitive part of your make-up. When I'm with someone I love, or for whom I have strong feelings, it can be incredibly difficult to accept his sexual side. I loved Daniel deeply but I often rejected physical intimacy. If I hadn't had such difficulties I might not have lost him. Now I accept that as part of my past and I have no regrets. But I understand that it is very difficult for a partner to accept sexual rejection without feeling hurt.

For a long time I have avoided relationships because I feel this problem will recur and I will leave myself open to being hurt again. And I will cause hurt. So I live a promiscuous life. If relationships are not to work then how else do I have any sort of a decent sex-life? It's easy to criticize, but many people who have been abused lead promiscuous lifestyles for all kinds of reasons.

I used to think that if someone knew everything about me he wouldn't really want me as a boyfriend. Today I think somewhat more of myself than that, but I still prefer to keep things casual. I have no moral problem with promiscuity and no guilt either. In fact these days I enjoy the lifestyle I should have been living years ago. Sexual activity can be invigorating, especially with someone new. Sometimes I feel like I'm twenty-one again, living life to the fullest. Other times good sex makes me feel appreciated and approved of and maybe because of my history I need that more than might otherwise be the case. The effects of child abuse don't stop with childhood.

Daniel. What can I say? He didn't get in touch despite promising to do so on that last night in my flat. In December 2000 I sent him a Christmas card and apologized for the hurt that my drinking must have caused him in our relationship. I didn't include my contact details because I didn't want him to think I was trying to provoke a response. It had been four and a half years, after all: if he'd really wanted to contact me he could have asked old friends in London.

On visits to London I always wondered what would happen if we met by chance. Just after Christmas 2001 I was there for a long weekend with my friend Noel Kennedy. It started brilliantly: on the first night we went to the Village in Soho and I was thrilled to have a chat with Boy George on his way back from the loo. I told him I had tickets for his musical, *Taboo*, and would be back to see it in February. He is the one addiction I still allow myself.

On Saturday night we went to a club, Heaven. There was a fantastic atmosphere that night. After dancing for a while I stood on the balcony overlooking the dance-floor and watched all the gorgeous boys. Behind me people were using a fire exit to come from the Dakota Room which is all R&B and a very hot room to dance in. For no reason I turned and my eyes were glued to the fire exit as people came through one by one.

Then I saw him. It had been six and a half years.

'Oh my God,' I said to Noel. 'Oh my God, it's Daniel.' But I didn't look to see his reaction. My eyes were fixed on Daniel.

I touched his arm. 'Hi, Daniel.'

With all the lights he couldn't see me. Then he did.

'Oh. My. God. I don't believe it.'

I could see he was shocked. He couldn't believe I looked so well and so healthy. He had hardly changed.

'This is Noel. He knows all about you,' I said.

'Everything?' he said.

'Just the truth,' I said, more sarcastically than I meant to.

We got past the bitchy moment and chatted. He said his parents would love to see me.

'No thanks.' I couldn't help myself.

He never got the card I'd sent the previous Christmas. His parents had sold the family home and moved from north to west London.

He phoned the following day. I cancelled my plans for the evening and we met in the Village – our haunt from years earlier – and then we went to Chinatown for dinner. It was so strange sitting chatting to him, like going back in time. Yet I was a different person. I said I was sorry for everything. Daniel said he was sorry he hadn't kept in touch; he didn't think I'd want to talk to him again.

He drove me back to Dolphin Square in Pimlico where I was staying – just a minute away from my old flat. We had driven those roads together hundreds of times in the past. I never thought we'd do it again. I think I was in shock. I made him get out of the car at Dolphin Square and gave him the biggest hug ever.

We've chatted frequently on the phone ever since and e-mail each other lots. It's good to be in touch with him again and I'm happy to love him as part of my past.

When I applied for the priesthood I really thought I was an ideal candidate, despite the abuse. Perhaps the character assessment showed otherwise. Maybe there were signs that something was wrong, although the psychologist who ana-lysed it didn't seem to think so.

Could it be that I wasn't religious or pious enough? I wanted to serve the people and God through the Catholic Church, which I loved and was very proud of. Was the emphasis wrong – too much on Church and not enough on God? Whatever happened to 'God calls in many ways'?

Now I can see that I might not have made a very good priest. As my depression and anxiety worsened over the years I would have found it very difficult to be all things to all people, twenty-four hours a day. And that was the kind of priest I planned on being.

I haven't had any desire to be a priest for many years, though that's not to say that my vocation was not █████

But a vocation has to be nurtured or it dies ████

soon after Father Brennan told me I wasn't suitab██

priesthood. My faith in Catholicism and in God was desu██

The very idea that the man who had abused me was more

suitable for priesthood than me was just too much of a hypo-

crisy for me to live with. I regret that I wasted my entire youth

on a vocation that was never realized, on a Church which

turned me away and shielded evil.

I am fortunate to have a spiritual life today that is not

connected with either the God or the religion I grew up with.

A power greater than myself keeps me well and sober. That's

all I know. I stay sober for all of my days, today, and that took

some getting used to. Staying sober every day can be difficult

after so many years of escaping from reality and myself. It has

been a struggle but I know I have grown so much by looking

at every aspect of my life and learning to accept and love

myself as I am. That doesn't mean there is no room for change.

A friend tells me that pain is the cornerstone of growth and

this sounds right to me. Sometimes it seems that I will only

embrace change when the status quo hurts too much.

I think I'm less sensitive today. The paralysing bouts of

anxiety and nervousness have almost gone. I can still be fearful

but the fear rarely wins out and now I do things I'm afraid of

and become stronger as a consequence. It's a job for life. I

know the world doesn't revolve around me, I'm just here

playing my part – but I have a right to be here and my part is

as good as anyone else's.

I feel better for having gone public and spoken out. And

writing everything down has helped more than I thought it

could. Every person I've spoken to, who has been sexually

abused as a child, is delighted about this book. For many of

them I haven't just told my own story but, to some extent,

theirs as well. I believe – I hope – that as more people speak out, even if not publicly, people with a tendency to abuse children will realize that the chances of being caught one day have risen so much that it's a risk too great to take.

Although I still carry many of the effects of child abuse, I no longer consider myself a victim. I've done something about it. I've turned it around. Father Payne is now the victim, the victim of his own actions. Now he's the one with the cross to bear.

# Appendix

1. Letter to Archbishop Desmond Connell, 5 April 1993

Dear Archbishop,

It would indeed be deplorable if you were not already somewhat aware of some of the contents of this letter. However, I wish to furnish you with all of the following information.

I was brought up and lived in the parish of Cabra, Dublin 7. From a very young age, I had a very strong desire to be a priest and this desire has influenced the course of my life for as far back as I can remember. As an altar boy at Christ the King Church, Cabra, I came into contact with Fr Ivan Payne, PC, who was a chaplain to our parish while having a full-time position at the Marriage Tribunal Section of Archbishop's House.

As a result of this contact, I was subsequently sexually molested and abused by Fr Payne. This abuse lasted approximately three years beginning when I was aged eleven/twelve and occurring on a weekly basis. This abuse has had serious and lasting effects upon me. The story of the above emerged when, in a very distressed state, I spoke to my Guidance Counsellor at my school (St Declan's College, Navan Road, Dublin). My counsellor then approached the Church authorities. As I understand it, Bishop D. O'Mahony, Monsignor A. Stenson and others were involved and Fr Payne was eventually moved to Sutton.

In the same year as I sat my Leaving Certificate, I approached

Fr Corry Brennan, vocations director, with a view to becoming a priest. I was told to go and get some work experience which I did at a frozen foods factory in Coolock. The following year I made a serious application to Clonliffe College to become a priest. I sat the standard examination and was subsequently assessed by a member of staff at Belfield, Dublin, who told me I could expect to see myself at Clonliffe the following September. Later, Fr Brennan was to tell me, without explanation, that I was not suitable for the priesthood. Needless to say, I was absolutely shattered by this.

In the years since, I have tried to live a normal life but I have found this extremely difficult, the effects of child abuse have never left me and I am hurting badly.

In June 1991, I consulted my solicitors, Gallagher and Shatter, for a view on my rights to sue Fr Payne for the damages which I have suffered. I wanted justice. I wanted to seek an acknowledgement from the Church that I have suffered at the hands of Fr Payne and I wanted compensation.

My solicitors wrote to Fr Payne on 25 March 1992 and a reply was received from the Church's solicitors, Arthur O'Hagan, on 14 April 1992 requesting details of the loss sustained by me. We confirmed in September 1992 that we were in receipt of a medical report. Not until 18 January 1993 did the Church solicitors agree to a meeting at the Four Courts, Dublin. On this occasion they said they needed a medical report of their own, which they could have asked for at any time since March 1992 but did not.

Despite the obvious pain it would cause, I agreed to a further medical report; hard to believe though it is, [no such arrangement for a medical assessment has been made] despite the passing of almost three months. In view of this, I have informed my solicitors that my consent for this second assessment to take place should be considered withdrawn with effect from 18 April 1993.

Archbishop, I have to tell you that as from 18 April 1993 I can no longer assure the anonymity of Fr Payne and Bishop O'Mahony. From that date, many options will be open to me and I intend to pursue every one of them.

From a very young age, I have suffered nothing but hurt and pain at the hands of the Catholic Church and what was once a very strong faith has been battered to bits.

Unless there is a radical change in some people's attitudes, which seems most unlikely, this matter is bound to move to the public domain. In such circumstances, I will not tolerate the Church authorities issuing statements to the effect that had they known about the proceedings pending against Fr Payne the whole matter would have been handled differently. I have now effectively closed that loophole because now, Archbishop, you do know.

Time is not exactly on your side, but I do invite you to take the opportunity to respond to all I have said.

Yours sincerely,

Andrew Madden

2. Letter to Cardinal Cahal Daly, 15 August 1995

Dear Cardinal Daly,

I would be most surprised if my name was not already known to you, however I will briefly put my correspondence into some context.

I am the person who was sexually abused by a Dublin priest on a weekly basis for three years beginning when I was aged eleven. I am now the first person on record in this country (as far as we know) to make a claim for damages after such abuse and received £27,500 nominal compensation for my continued pain and suffering.

Earlier this year I gave my story to Colm Keena at the *Irish Press* and subsequently gave an interview to Joe Duffy on the *Gay Byrne* radio show, some of which I presume was brought to your attention, as indeed it should have been.

More recently my identity was revealed, with my consent, by the *Sunday World* and the *Sunday Express*.

Over recent months questions have been put to the Irish Catholic Church which the Church has refused to answer. These questions were asked on my behalf by various British and Irish newspapers and sometimes referred to my case specifically and other times questions were asked in more general terms. On no occasion have these questions been answered to any satisfaction, which is a total disgrace; the notion that because your positions of authority and power in public life are so assured, and that the Church is not account-able to the public in any way, should allow you to show such disregard for people like me who rightfully challenge the way you conduct your affairs is a clear indication of a level of arrogance which needs to be checked.

I am meeting Bishop O'Mahony on Wednesday, 16 August 1995; Bishop O'Mahony has already made it clear that he will discuss my own personal welfare and will also address some of the complaints I made on radio about being treated so badly when I made my own application to the priesthood some years ago. He has also made it clear that he will not answer any questions about the priest who abused me (the identity of whom I presume you troubled yourself to take the time to ascertain); nor will he answer any general questions about the way the Catholic Church deals with paedophile priests; Bishop O'Mahony has suggested that my questions should be addressed to someone else and I have decided that as Head of the Catholic Church in Ireland you have a moral responsibility to answer my questions.

Can you tell me:

(a) What treatment do paedophile priests receive after they have admitted their offences?

(b) How effective is this treatment?

(c) How do you know it is effective?

(d) How do you know that it is safe to put a priest with a record of child abuse back into the community in a position of trust without putting other children at risk?

(e) Can you please explain Archbishop Connell's recent comment in a private letter to my mother that priests with a record of child abuse are 'monitored' (a practice I imagine must be very difficult) – please don't advise me to revert back to the Archbishop as you are his superior and I expect you to answer the question.

(f) How many priests in Ireland are currently facing allegations of child abuse and indeed how many have there been in, say, the last ten to twenty years and how many of those are currently serving priests?

Your response will be something of an indication to me as to how the Church may have changed in recent times and I await such response eagerly.

Yours sincerely,

Andrew Madden

3. Letter from Cardinal Cahal Daly, 18 September 1995

Dear Mr Madden,

I write further to my letter of 18 August [a letter of acknowledgement] in response to your letter of 15 August last.

I wish to emphasize again my concern for you. I am aware of the great hurt and distress which you still feel.

You have asked a number of questions about how Church authorities are responding to the problem of a priest who has abused and I will try to answer your questions as best I can:

(a) *What treatment do paedophile priests receive after they have admitted their offences?*

Priests who have admitted offences are normally required to undergo evaluation by specialists in the field of child sexual offending. The course of treatment followed will be that advised by the specialist. Our concern is that the offender receive the most effective treatment, not only for his own benefit but to protect others in the future.

(b)/(c) *How effective is this treatment? How do you know it is effective?*

Not only is our society, including the Catholic Church, growing in its understanding of the crime of child sexual abuse, but the medical profession has also made considerable strides in the past few years in attempting to understand and treat both. Those strides have revealed how misunderstood the problem of child sexual abuse was in the past. My understanding of the modern treatment programmes is that they normally involve a number of important elements such as: admission of guilt; breaking through denial; developing victim empathy; developing the capacity for peer relationships; a commitment on the part of the perpetrator to a life-long road to recovery.

I understand that many perpetrators in modern treatment programmes make substantial progress on these issues. The effectiveness of the treatment requires clinical appraisal in each and every case.

(d) *How do you know that it is safe to put a priest with a record of child abuse back into the community in a position of trust without putting other children at risk?*

In deciding whether to re-admit a priest who has offended to active ministry, a Bishop is guided by the clinical advice he receives, which will include advice on aftercare, review and appropriate supervision. A Bishop will also have careful regard to pastoral considerations attendant on any particular appointment.

(e) *Can you please explain Archbishop Connell's recent comment in a private letter to my mother that priests with a record of child abuse are 'monitored' (a practice I imagine must be very difficult) – please don't advise me to revert back to the Archbishop as you are his superior and I expect you to answer the question.*

It would be presumptuous of me to offer an explanation of Archbishop Connell's response to your mother. However, when a decision is made to re-admit an offender to priestly ministry, such re-admission will usually be conditional upon clinical aftercare, supervision and review. The bishop and priests amongst others will wholeheartedly participate in this process where appropriate.

(f) *How many priests in Ireland are currently facing allegations of child abuse and indeed how many have there been in, say, the last ten to twenty years and how many of those are currently serving priests?*

Allegations have been made against a number of priests in recent times. This is a matter of deep concern to me. Many of these allegations are of wrongdoing a considerable time ago and each had its own particular circumstances. I am not aware of the number of allegations recently or in the past.

Again I wish to express to you my sincere and deep sorrow for your hurt and distress.

Yours sincerely,

+ Cahal B. Card. Daly

Archbishop of Armagh

4. Letter sent to leaders of each of Ireland's twenty-six dioceses, 1 July 1996

I write with reference to the report of the Irish Catholic Bishop's Advisory Committee on Child Sexual Abuse by Priests and Religious published on 30 January 1996. As someone who was sexually abused as a child by a priest I was very interested in the document and am keen to know to what extent it has been implemented. In this regard I would be most pleased if you could furnish me with the following information on your Diocese:

(a) Have you accepted that the guidelines should be implemented in full in your diocese or have you opted for an alternative protocol?

(b) If you have opted for an alternative could you please supply me with details of same?

(c) Assuming you have accepted the guidelines can you please tell me who you have appointed as your Delegate, Support Person, and Advisor and which people have you chosen to form your Advisory Panel?

(d) To what extent have your Delegate, Support Person and Advisor received appropriate training since their appointments?

(e) What steps has your Delegate taken to promote awareness and understanding of child sexual abuse among the priests of the Diocese or members of the religious congregation?

(f) Can you guarantee that all allegations of child abuse by priests or religious will be reported to the civil authorities or will this action only be taken once the Diocese has established for itself that such allegations have the essence of truth about them?

(g) Finally, are you in a position to indicate the number of priests who, following allegations of child abuse in the past, were moved on to new parishes possibly having 'received treatment' between the time of your appointment as Bishop and the publication of the guidelines, and if not why not?

5. Letter from Michael Murphy, Bishop of Cork and Ross, 4 July 1996

Dear Mr Madden

I wish to acknowledge receipt of your letter of 1 July, for which I thank you. I regret to hear that you have been the subject of abuse by a priest, while a child. I do hope that you have received appropriate help.

It is a matter of public record that the Irish Catholic Bishops accepted the report of their Advisory Committee on Child Sexual Abuse by Priests and Religious. I assure that any such complaints which have been received in these dioceses have always been dealt with appropriately. Particular attention is given to the complainant and the accused, with due regard to the rights of all concerned and the requirements of civil and canon law. That has been, and continues to be, my policy.

With prayerful good wishes,

I remain

Yours in Christ

+ Michael Murphy

Bishop of Cork & Ross

6. Letter on behalf of Archbishop Desmond Connell, 11 July 1996

Dear Mr Madden,

The Archbishop, who is away at present, has asked me to reply to your letter of 1 July.

The Archbishop has directed that the Framework is to be implemented in full in the Archdiocese of Dublin and has taken the necessary steps to implement this decision. All the appointments required by the Framework have been made. An Advisory Board consisting of eleven members under a lay chairperson has been established. In making appointments the Archbishop has regard for the professional competence required for the fulfilment of the tasks to be fulfilled.

The Archbishop has fully implemented the reporting policy outlined in 2.2.1 of the Framework Document.

In determining the future of any priest against whom allegations have been made, the Archbishop has always been guided by the advice received from those professionally competent to give it.

With every kind wish,

[the letter was signed by a priest of the Archbishop's staff]

7. Letter from Jim Cantwell, Director of the Catholic Press and Information Office, 10 July 1996

Dear Mr Madden

Bishops have been in touch with me concerning the letter of 1 July which you have sent to each of them seeking certain information regarding the implementation in their dioceses of procedures recommended in the Report of the Bishops' Advisory Committee on Child Sexual Abuse by Priests and

Religious, Framework for a Church Response. The bishops understand your concern about the issue of child sexual abuse which has caused you hurt and distress. At their behest, I have undertaken to respond to your letter in a manner which reflects the current situation in Irish dioceses. I write not only as information officer for the bishops but as one who was a member of the Advisory Committee.

I can state that each diocese in Ireland has adopted as its protocol the guidelines recommended in the Framework document.

Each diocese has put in place the structures recommended for implementation of the protocol. Each has also appointed the personnel recommended in the Framework document. The name of the Delegate appointed in each diocese has been made public; the Delegate is responsible for ensuring the protocol is implemented when a complaint of child sexual abuse is made against a priest, so it is important that his identity is known locally. The names of the Support Person, the Advisor and the members of the Advisory Panel have not generally been publicized in order to protect their privacy.

A thorough programme of training for personnel who have the responsibility of implementing the protocol has been initiated and some training sessions have already taken place.

The active promotion among diocesan priests and religious of awareness and understanding of child sexual abuse is of critical importance and has, in fact, been going on since at least 1994. All dioceses – either individually or co-operatively on a regional basis – have held information days designed specifically for priests or religious. Many of these information days have involved health care personnel and police, as well as experts in the counselling of victims and offenders. More-over, in conjunction with the publication of the Framework document, bishops held information days for their priests at which members of the Advisory Committee explained the thinking behind the Framework document. Each priest in the country received a copy of the Framework document, together with a summary of its contents prepared by this office. You will note that paragraph 9.2.2 of the document recommends that information days or seminars for priests and religious should continue to be arranged and should be followed up with the provision of new and additional information as and when it becomes available.

Each diocese has accepted as part of its protocol the clear reporting practice recommended in paragraphs 2.2.1–2.2.3 of the Framework document. Any suspicion or knowledge that a priest has sexually abused a child will be reported to the civil authorities. This reporting practice goes beyond the require-ments under statute law both in the Republic of Ireland and Northern Ireland, but is very much in line with the guidelines adopted by major child care agencies in both jurisdictions. The recommendation of the Advisory Committee on reporting policy followed the most detailed discussion of all the issues involved, and particularly of the very sensitive question of confidentiality which may arise in the case of a complaint by an adult of abuse during childhood. The Framework document states that 'in making its recommendations in regard to reporting, the Advisory Committee considers to be paramount the safety and protection of children and the need to prevent, where possible, further abuse' (2.2.6).

It is policy for dioceses to take seriously any complaints made against priests. Within the past decade there has been a growing public awareness worldwide of the nature and the impact of child sexual abuse within society generally. Catholic Church authorities in Ireland recognized the need for dioceses and religious congregations to put in place appropriate pro-cedures for dealing with complaints against priests or religious.

The clear and comprehensive guidelines recommended by the Bishops' Advisory Committee are intended i) to enable victims of child sexual abuse by priests and religious to disclose their experiences in the expectation of a sensitive, caring response, and ii) to have the protection and welfare of children as their first and paramount concern.

Concerning the specific question g) in your letter I am not in a position to provide the information you request. The criteria for decisions about the future of priests and religious known to have offended are clearly laid down in Chapter 7 of the Framework document. In regard to receipt of complaints the document states (2.2.5) that 'undertakings of confidentiality should not be given but rather the information should be expressly received within the terms of this reporting policy and on the basis that *only those who need to know will be told*' (my italics).

With every good wish,

Yours sincerely,

Jim Cantwell

8. Letter from An Taoiseach, Bertie Ahern, 9 June 1998

Dear Mr Madden,

Thank you for your letter of 4 March 1998 to the Taoiseach Mr Bertie Ahern, TD, requesting a public inquiry into the Catholic Church's handling of allegations of sexual abuse of children by priests and other religious in Ireland.

The Taoiseach fully appreciates the deep personal hurt caused to you and to others who have been sexually abused as children and has been greatly offended by the nature and extent of those outrages.

He has asked me to explain to you that, although he has

great sympathy for your position, it would not be appropriate for the Government to establish a public inquiry into the way in which the Catholic Church handled allegations of sexual abuse. The difficulties lie in the impracticality of such a tribunal and the fact that the Catholic Church is not a public body.

Unlike the other instances of tribunals and inquiries referred to by you, a tribunal of the kind you have in mind would be uniquely difficult (tribunals of inquiry can only be established, under the relevant legislation, for the purpose of inquiring into definite matters of urgent public importance).

In all the other cases there have either been very definite allegations of misconduct against identifiable individuals or, as in the case of the planning tribunal, there are clearly identifiable public bodies. The tribunal proposed by you, if it was to be comprehensive and effective, would have to be open to allegations against an unspecified, but clearly a very large, number of bodies and people and would have to relate to an unspecified period of time, going back most likely in some cases thirty, forty or more years.

There would also be an intrinsic, and probably legally challengeable, unfairness in a process which focused on the Catholic Church and abuse by clergy. Although such cases are the ones which come most frequently to attention there are also cases involving lay people and it is difficult to see why a tribunal should be prevented from hearing evidence relating to abuse in institutions owned or managed by other denominational or secular authorities. The scale of such inquiries would be very great indeed; so great in fact it is difficult to see how they could ever be effective.

It is also necessary to address the view that the Catholic Church is in some sense a public body by proxy, into the affairs of which it would be appropriate to hold a public inquiry.

The Church in no sense acts as the agent of the State in

matters of education and child care, and the State has not conferred control over broad areas of education and child care as you suggest in your letter. The position of the various denominational churches in matters relating to education and health was already a well established fact at the foundation of the State and that position was given constitutional recognition and protection in 1937 by the citizens of the State.

The approach adopted by the State, since its foundation, in regard to education and child care was both pragmatic and based on the wishes of the people – it provided public funds to the institutions which had traditionally provided these services. In doing so it did not and could not, because of the constitutionally guaranteed autonomy of the churches, seek to supervise the day-to-day operation of schools and other institutions. It is not accepted that the approach can be held to have contributed to abuse.

While as explained a tribunal of inquiry is not considered as appropriate or practical to the issues of child abuse, the Government are fully committed to the investigation and prosecution by the statutory agencies of those who are responsible for these dreadful crimes against children.

The Government also consider that the best way to reduce the incidence of child abuse is to develop child and family support services, including programmes to raise awareness among children about abuse and of the importance of confiding in a trusted adult if abuse occurs. A major expansion of child and family support services has taken place in recent years to support the implementation of the Child Care Act, 1991, and further developments are planned e.g. mandatory reporting; discussion paper on sexual offences and the Child Trafficking and Pornography Bill presently before the Oireachtas.

The Taoiseach has asked me to assure you of his personal

commitment to maintain progress in the development of a modern child care system which will hopefully reduce the pain and suffering which too many of our children have experienced at the hands of adults.

The Government are committed to keeping this whole area under review particularly in assessing, in the light of developments, any further measures which would be likely to prove useful in ensuring that the type of abuse in question could be better guarded against in the future.

The Taoiseach hopes that this reply clarifies the Government's position in relation to the important issues which you raised with him.

Your sincerely,

[the signature was illegible]

Private secretary to the Taoiseach